Praise for *The Gandhiana Jones Project*

"This book is a distillation of years of experimentation with issues of meaning and purpose. Mr. Gandhi famously said, 'Life is but an endless series of experiments.' Joe Kelly shows us precisely how to perform these life-changing experiments. Read every page!"

—Stephen Cope, founder, Kripalu Institute for Extraordinary Living, and bestselling author of *The Great Work of Your Life*

"If you want step-by-step instructions and exercises on how to live a more fulfilling life, read *The Gandhiana Jones Project.*"

—Azim Jamal, bestselling coauthor of *The Power of Giving*

"This empowering book will inspire you to reach for your dreams."

—Robert Maurer, PhD, bestselling author of *One Small Step Can Change Your Life*

THE
GANDHIANA
JONES
PROJECT

AN 8-WEEK COURSE IN BECOMING THE
CHANGE YOU WANT TO SEE IN THE WORLD

JOE KELLY

WONDERWELL

Library of Congress Control Number: 2021914252

ISBN 978-1-63756-010-5 (paperback)
ISBN 978-1-63756-011-2 (EPUB)

Editor: Joanna Henry
Cover design and interior design: Morgan Krehbiel
Typesetting: Paul Dotey
Cover images: bullwhip by iStock/stevecoleimages; beads by iStock/jackof
Author photo: Neil Goodes

Published by Wonderwell in Los Angeles, CA
www.wonderwell.press

WONDERWELL

Distributed in the US by Publishers Group West and
in Canada by Publishers Group Canada

Printed and bound in Canada

To Dad,
who nudged me toward a higher path.
Your memory whispers: stay the course.

CONTENTS

APPENDIX A: ADVICE AND POINTERS

APPENDIX B: BIBLIOGRAPHY

INTRODUCTION

//

**Our greatest ability as humans is not to change
the world; but to change ourselves.**
– MAHATMA GANDHI

"CAN YOU NAME SOME GREAT CHANGE-MAKERS IN THE WORLD?"
I ask my class. I'm standing in front of thirty fresh-faced university stu-
dents on their first day of the academic year, a whiteboard behind me.
Hands begin to raise. I start writing.

"Mother Teresa."

"Nelson Mandela."

"Martin Luther King Jr."

"Rosa Parks."

"Mahatma Gandhi."

It's a lineup of iconic historical figures that make the list every year
when I give the students this exercise.

"These are all people who are remembered because they've had a huge
impact on the world," I say. "And I'm sure you could name many more. But
now, I want to hear about people you've actually met. They don't have to
be well known, but they've made a real difference in their own communities. Regular people." The list that follows is quite different.

"My aunt Phyllis started a community garden."

"A guy in my neighborhood puts on a block party every year that
raises money for homeless people."

1

"My fifth-grade teacher got our whole class connected to a group of kids in Uganda."

"These examples," I say, "are all ordinary people who've done extraordinary things. On the surface, they may not seem as great as Gandhi, but everyone on both of these lists has done something to better the world, whether they're famous or not. So, what qualities do you think they possess that you don't?" I look out at a sea of furrowed eyebrows. "How did they get to be change-makers?"

It's a rhetorical question. I know they're here to find out how. I've been teaching the course, called Project Change, for several years now—and it all began in an elevator.

It was 2013, and I had been working as a college professor for some time. My watershed moment came while waiting for the elevator up to my third-floor office. In the past, I'd always grumbled about people who use the elevator to go up just a few floors. Didn't they see a golden opportunity to get some exercise? But now, I was one of them. I had always thought of myself as an active person and someone who used every moment of my day wisely. *When did I stop taking the stairs?* I wondered. I couldn't remember. *How did you let this happen?* I glanced down at the doughnut in my hand.

From the outside, taking an elevator may seem inconsequential. But from the inside, it felt much bigger. What I saw in that moment of stark clarity was that I was not living in alignment with my values. One small change in my behavior had impacted my life negatively, in perhaps more than one way. I was slightly overweight and grumpy about it, at the very least. In my head, I heard another question: *What if you made just one positive change in your life, right now?* I didn't think twice—I took the stairs.

This incident triggered a thought process that lasted throughout the week. I began to see the larger picture of my life, and I didn't like what I was seeing. In debt, single, and feeling disconnected from the people around me, I was on autopilot. Something had gone off the rails in my life, and it would take a conscious effort to put it right.

I continued to take the stairs daily until I was sprinting up them. One morning, as I burst through the door of my office, a saying I'd seen on a bumper sticker popped into my head: "Be the change you want to see in the world." It was from Mahatma Gandhi.

This gentle man had lived very simply and owned very little, working tirelessly for economic, religious, and gender equality in India and eventually becoming the leader of a political movement that overthrew British rule. His efforts catalyzed the civil rights movements in North America and across the globe that began midway through the twentieth century. This was a change-maker the likes of which the world had rarely seen. I thought about how he had conducted his life and wondered what lessons I might draw for my own.

I'm not going to lie; having Gandhi as a role model seemed a tall order. He was so selfless and accomplished so much, but—and I don't mean to sound flippant—did he enjoy himself? I still liked my cappuccinos, steaks, movies, vacations...I found myself wondering if sacrificial duty was a prerequisite to living as a change-maker.

I began to think about other people I'd admired over the course of my life and remembered my very first larger-than-life role model: Indiana Jones. I was nine in 1981 when the film *Raiders of the Lost Ark* was released, and I can remember breathlessly watching Indiana, the daring archaeologist, as he braved unknown worlds, cracked his whip, and saved the world from evil. I idolized him. His combination of smarts, raw courage, passion, humor, and style was incredibly appealing to me. And it still is. If you can do good things *and* live an adventurous life, then count me in!

At first glance, my two role models couldn't have had less in common—until I reconsidered the quote, "Be the change you want to see in the world."

Gandhi didn't set out trying to be an influential leader or attempting to get others to change. He started with himself. He lived in perfect alignment with his values. So did Indy, for that matter. This common ground seemed like a good starting place for me as well.

With Gandhi and Indy as my role models, I decided to embark on a yearlong experiment, determined to make positive and meaningful changes in my life. I would make change, do it authentically, and have fun along the way. Every month, I selected a new challenge for a different area of my life: leadership, service, health, the environment, technology, spirituality, and so on. Being an educator and researcher, I also developed a systematic method by which to measure the results. I couldn't wait to get started.

One month, I spent an hour in nature every day. Another month, I unplugged from technology. Yet another month, I walked everywhere I needed to go. Before long, I was shedding pounds, paying off my debt, and learning new skills. I felt great. That was to be expected, I suppose, but I hadn't anticipated that improving my life would lead to others feeling great, too. It was like a positive feedback loop. My positive effects on others enhanced my own happiness and sense of meaning. The behavior changes I was making rippled out into my community and then back to me. And once I began directing my challenges outward, like performing deliberate acts of kindness every day for a month, I found these things had a longer-lasting impact on my own sense of well-being than hitting my target weight or paying off my last outstanding bill. By the end of the year, my experiment with change had revealed a lot.

We are indeed more interdependent than we realize. We are not alone, tending the gardens of our lives in isolation. We are all connected. What we put out into the world determines what we get back and, ultimately, how we feel inside.

Over the years that followed, I continued this journey. I walked a path of self-discovery rich with challenges, triumphs, and revelations, evolving my approach through further experimentation, research, interviews, and writing. I had been teaching at the university for some years now and realized that I might be able to apply my learning to create a roadmap for my students. So, I overhauled one of my courses, and Project Change was born. Which brings me back to the whiteboard...

"So, you admire Gandhi, Mother Teresa, and Rosa Parks, plus the folks in your own lives who've all done good in the world. Those are some real change-makers." The students nod in agreement. "Well, what about someone like Indiana Jones?" I hear a collective pause. I can tell they're not sure what to think.

"Let me share a secret," I say conspiratorially. "Being a change-maker isn't just about sacrifice and martyrdom. You can fill your days with things that bring you happiness *and* serve others. Pleasure matters. Fun matters. Adventure matters." Now the students are excited. "What if you could be both—Gandhi and Indiana Jones?"

Although they want to believe it, I can tell they don't. Yet. But what they discover over the course of the semester is that it *is possible*. What is important when emulating these figures is not what they achieved, but how they did it. They worked from the inside out. They lived authentically. They lived with purpose and passion and courage. They followed their hearts.

Throughout the semester, my students learned step-by-step how to be the change they wanted to see in the world. They emerged from the course equipped with new tools, resources, and ways of thinking. They learned to identify and apply their personal values, passions, and skills to their acts of service; and the results they achieved surpassed everyone's wildest imaginings. Even mine.

All of this experience eventually made its way into the book you're now reading.

Are you ready to start your own adventure?

Don't worry if Mahatma Gandhi or Indiana Jones don't resonate for you. Perhaps your role-model mash-up would look more like Oprah Winfrey meets Hermione Granger, or the Dalai Lama meets T'Challa, or Marcus Aurelius meets Katniss Everdeen—whatever works for you! As you will see in the coming weeks, the Gandhiana Jones Project is not a cookie-cutter model to apply to your life. You will be challenged to delve deep inside in order to chart your own unique course for change.

My hope is that you will enjoy this process and, as you engage with it, ignite your own sense of purpose; become more aligned with your values and vision; and feel more confident, connected, and fulfilled. I trust you will find inspiration in these pages to spark change in your own life and in the world around you. Let's go, Gandhiana Jones!

HOW TO USE
THIS BOOK

///

**If you want to be a good archaeologist,
you gotta get out of the library!**
– INDIANA JONES*

THIS BOOK IS DESIGNED TO TAKE YOU ON AN EIGHT-WEEK JOURNEY of self-discovery and change. I have included practical research results along with real-life accounts of people who have all found their own unique way to live as change-makers. I've drawn from my personal experience as well.

The eight weeks are divided into two parts. Following in the wisdom of Gandhi—by transforming ourselves, we can transform the world around us—we begin with our own inward development in Part One. And following in the wisdom of Indy, it's going to be fun. In these first four weeks, we'll explore the four main principles of the Gandhiana Jones Project:

- Values
- Passion
- Skills
- Service

*Indiana Jones and the Kingdom of the Crystal Skull (2008)

7

I will guide you through a step-by-step process of identifying and implementing each one of these principles in your life. You will learn how to uncover your values, nurture your passions, sharpen your skills, and be of service to the world.

In Part Two, we'll use the final four weeks to focus on moving outward and creating the change you want to see in the world. You will learn how to develop your vision and goals, engage people from your community to help you achieve them, and blast through any obstacles that stand in the way. You will also learn how to bolster your inner reserves for the journey ahead.

Learning by Doing

Throughout the book, you'll find a number of exercises and challenges that will help you put the material into practice.

Let's say you want to get in better shape, so you read a book on fitness. It would be ludicrous to think you could achieve your health goals by reading that book and doing nothing else; you must get in the gym and sweat. The same thing applies to this book. Its contents are useful, but to achieve results, you must get out there and practice. Think of the book's exercises and challenges as a training regime for getting your whole self—body, mind, heart, and soul—into better shape.

Written Exercises. These exercises, included at the end of each weekly lesson, will help you to dig into the concepts from that week and apply them to your own life. Most of them take about fifteen minutes and should ideally be done with a pen and paper right after you've finished reading. This way, the material is still fresh in your mind. Many exercises will require some brainstorming, so I have included some tips for effective brainstorming in the Appendix.

Weekly Challenges. Each week's lesson concludes with a weekly challenge. With these, you will be asked to undertake a thirty-minute activity daily for seven days. There are eight challenges in all—one for each week—and I encourage you to do them back-to-back over a span of eight weeks for greatest benefit.

To maximize your learning, I recommend that you set aside time after completing each weekly challenge to journal and reflect on your experiences. I've provided a series of questions in the Appendix to help guide you through this process.

In the classroom, most types of growth and development happen after hours, when students are working on their projects and applying what they've learned. This is known as experiential learning (or "learning by doing"). The same holds true for this book; your progress will take place when you put what you're learning into practice, and if you take the time to put in this work, you'll be blown away by your own results.

PART ONE

THE FOUR PRINCIPLES

WEEK 1

VALUES: FOLLOWING YOUR COMPASS

Your values become your destiny.
– MAHATMA GANDHI

Compass. I need a compass.
– INDIANA JONES*

CHRISTMAS DAY IN BALI, DRINKING PIÑA COLADAS ON THE BEACH —that was how I planned to spend the last part of my writing sabbatical in 2014. I had been working hard on the Indonesian island for nearly six months, and as a reward, I was finally going to hit the beach, sweet tropical cocktail in hand, and take in the white sand, blue sky, and fresh air.

But the sweetness in my holiday plans turned bitter. I swapped out the cocktail for a plane ticket, the white sand for snow, as I rushed back to Canada just before Christmas to be by my dying father's side.

His death from cancer happened so quickly that it was difficult to

*Indiana Jones and the Kingdom of the Crystal Skull (2008)

13

process. I wasn't ready to say goodbye. I'm not sure more time together would have fixed that, but I was comforted by knowing I could be with him and that he was surrounded by loving family and friends right to the end. We even got to open some Christmas gifts with him on December 22, on what would turn out to be his last full day. This gave us all a shared experience of joy, though it was fleeting.

Two days after my father died, my family gathered for Christmas Day. To pay tribute to his spirit of playfulness and love of the outdoors, we drove to a small, secluded beach at a lakeside park not far from my parents' home in British Columbia's Okanagan Valley. It was a cold and clear day. The sun was out. The lake was still. The park was vacant except for our small group, and it was a peaceful setting for a somber occasion. We honored my dad with a short Irish blessing and a reading of the poem *Remember Me*, by David Harkins.

One of the stanzas in adaptations of the poem reads, "You can remember me and only that I have gone or you can cherish my memory and let it live on."

Taking the poem to heart, I spent several days after Christmas contemplating how to honor my father's memory and keep it alive. During this time of reflection, I kept coming back to one thing: my dad's integrity.

The expression "salt of the earth" comes to mind when I think of my dad. He was an honest, stand-up kind of guy—a natural provider who was fiercely loyal to his family and always there to help others, without asking anything in return. With Dad, actions spoke louder than words. His love was tacit but present in everything he did. His life was grounded in a core set of values that served as a strong inner compass: hard work, fairness, family, kindness, and stability all come to mind.

My father led by example rather than prescription, and through his actions, he taught me what it means to stay true to your values and live a life that's guided by a higher moral code. There was no better way to pay homage to his memory, I thought, than to model this way of living. I would stake claim to my own values, then take deliberate steps to live them out in my daily life. There was just one problem: I could name my father's values, but not my own. I wasn't even sure how to go about identifying them, let alone how to live a life based on them.

Where to start?

Trust Your Gut

With my father gone, I looked to another mentor—a man by the name of Marc Stoiber—for advice on how to uncover and align with my own values. I'd known Marc for several years and had turned to him for counsel on my professional goals on more than one occasion. He had been influential in my decision to take a writing sabbatical in Bali. Marc had taken his family there for an extended holiday, and when not home schooling his kids or surfing the local reef break, he hammered out his book *Didn't See It Coming*—a provocative yet fun-filled read that explores the advertising and marketing industry in a post-9/11 world.

While the term "adman" may bring to mind the outdated image of executives at a martini luncheon dreaming up slick taglines for flogging products that nobody needs, Marc is anything but. With his twenty-five years of advertising and marketing experience, Marc is a vocal critic of consumerism. He cares about what's being sold and how it's being sold to us, and his marketing work is deeply entwined with these values. He got there by trusting his gut.

In the early part of his career, Marc worked for big advertising agencies, using his creative talents to help clients peddle their products in the marketplace. Then he made what many people would consider a risky decision—he left a lucrative career to start his own small company that leveraged his marketing talent for the good of the consumer.

In an interview with me, Marc described with dramatic flair the exact moments the lights went on. While working to revive a stagnant advertising account for a brand of cleaning products, one of his team members entered the office with what looked like a rainbow of plastic bottles full of cleaning liquids, each in a different color. "Spring, summer, autumn, and winter scents!" he effused. This new angle on an old product was created to lure homemakers into purchasing four times a year, when they likely still had a perfectly good half-full bottle under the kitchen sink. You wouldn't want your floor smelling like summer when it was autumn, now, would you?

"That evening," Marc continued in his animated style, "I talked to my wife about the dim bulb of doubt that was glowing in my head. 'Does the world really need four more flavors of floor cleaner?' I asked. Her answer, a simple 'No,' pretty much ruined my life. Because when you work in advertising and you finally realize the world doesn't need what you're selling, you're screwed. As the bulb of doubt began to glow more brightly, I soon realized my days in Big Agencyland were numbered."

Leaving his agency and job security behind, Marc started on a new career path based on his principles rather than the size of his paycheck. He launched his own independent practice with a more ethical goal in mind: to help companies get ahead by building brands that are authentic, innovative, and sustainable.

"It took a long time to start paying attention to my values," Marc told me. "But now that I do, I feel a lot more balanced...like I have a foundation to stand on."

For Marc, it all comes down to the gut. Not your literal belly, of course, but that instinctive sense that is beyond thought or feeling yet informed by both. "Trust your gut," he told me. "Your head may well get you to more money and success. But at the end of the day, your gut makes you a better person. That's worth more than money."

According to Marc Stoiber, these feelings of inner turmoil can serve a useful purpose by signaling that your values have been compromised. Even if you haven't identified your values explicitly, they're always present—whether you're conscious of them or not—and you often instinctively know when aspects of your life are out of sync with them. "You will know you're on the right track," Marc told me, "when your gut doesn't keep poking you and reminding you that you're a phony."

In other words, you don't need to know how to name your values to know when you aren't living by them. This insight from Marc's story was my lightbulb moment. I saw the truth of it immediately as I thought back to a key turning point in my own career.

It was 2009, three years after I finished grad school, and I was working as a sustainability consultant at a midsize management consulting firm in

Vancouver. On paper, it was a fantastic job. The projects were interesting, the people were smart, I enjoyed a high level of autonomy, and I was well compensated. But I wasn't happy.

As with many professions, the holy grail of consulting is the billable hour. This means there is a lot of pressure to fill the working days with billable activities, and job performance is judged accordingly. Do well and there will be a lucrative bonus—along with a demand for even better results.

After the best-producing twelve months of my career, my target was increased by almost 100 percent. I didn't know whether to be flattered or insulted. Although I was surpassing quotas at work with success after success, my personal life was a complete mess. Here I was, helping my clients adopt sustainable business practices, but my work-life balance was so lopsided that it was toxic. My situation was akin to a financial planner buried under a mountain of personal debt, or a relationship counselor going through his third divorce.

My values and actions were in direct conflict, and the pangs of discontent were rumbling loudly for me—not only in my gut, but in my whole body. I was moody. I was in pain. Most weeks were capped off by a physical trifecta of tense muscles, eye strain, and a screaming headache that lingered into the weekend. Sundays were my sanctuary: that glorious sliver of time when I could finally relax and unwind. But the reprieve was short-lived. Like clockwork, right around suppertime, thoughts of Monday morning and the looming week ahead would begin to creep into my head and unsettle my mind. The vicious weekly cycle would begin anew.

I'm embarrassed to admit this now, but my first attempts to repair my condition were shallow and materialistic. I turned to self-indulgence to fill the void: buying things I didn't need, throwing money around at trendy bars and fancy restaurants, and chasing romantic partners who looked good on my arm but didn't connect with my soul. I even owned a convertible roadster, the ultimate symbol of overcompensation. But even in the roadster, I couldn't navigate my way out of the mess. My moral compass was spinning wildly, and I was lost—not to mention in a fair bit of debt.

I wish I could tell you that I had an earth-shattering epiphany one day, whereupon, realizing the error of my ways, I just up and quit my job to join some international aid organization. Alas, it wasn't that exciting. But maybe that's the point.

One day, I was cold called by a local college professor. The semester had just started, and he still needed someone to teach a course in his department. Did I want the job? I didn't hesitate. I said yes.

Later, all kinds of doubts came up. Would teaching be right for me? I would be taking a hefty pay cut from my job in the private sector, so how would I pay those credit card bills? And how, exactly, would this job be better aligned with my values? I didn't know. But what I did know was that I was unhappy. My life was out of alignment. And when the teaching job was offered to me, there was an immediate yes in my gut. It was time to listen to my instincts instead of my head. It required a big leap of faith, but I trusted my gut and jumped.

Uncovering Your Values

Listening to your gut is a great first step in uncovering your values, but it can only take you so far. It is kind of like playing the children's game I Spy, where you follow the hints (warmer or colder) as you tune in to your gut reaction in any situation and notice how you feel, letting your responses guide you. This will help you to determine whether you're getting closer to your values, but it can't identify them for you. It's an indirect route and one that requires you to try different paths, adjusting the course as you go along. That can take time, and there's no guaranteeing you will eventually stumble on what you're after.

I wanted to find the next step in moving from a place of living reactively, from my hidden values, to living proactively, from my identified values. The question I sought to answer was this: Is it possible to take a direct, active approach to uncovering your values?

In my search for an answer, I continued researching and interviewing individuals with demonstrated success in living according to their own values. In doing so, I discovered three effective methods for unearthing your core values: cutting back on some of the material things in your life, reflecting on peak experiences from your past, and identifying your role models.

LESS IS MORE

North America's great Interior Plains extend from Texas all the way to Canada, doglegging in the north through Montana into the Canadian province of Alberta. The southern part of that province is a wide-open expanse of prairie, bordered to the west by the Rocky Mountains and their foothills. The region is dry, averaging about twelve to fifteen inches of rain annually, and its semiarid climate makes it vulnerable to frequent and severe droughts, as well as unpredictable bursts of rain. In June 2014, southern Alberta received nearly eight inches of rainfall—roughly half its average annual allotment—in less than two days. The downpour triggered the worst flooding in the province's history, causing over $5 billion in damage and displacing more than 100,000 people throughout the region.

Julie Phillips was one of them. Julie, who lived in Calgary, Alberta, was moving into a new apartment in a pleasant riverside neighborhood when floodwaters rendered her new digs uninhabitable. Without a place to live, she accepted a friend's kind offer to stay in his guest room. She was lucky he had room for her, but there was no room for her *stuff*. Forced to downsize, she gave away the bulk of her possessions.

The experience left her shaken, but it also put her on a new trajectory. Less than a month later, Julie would take downsizing to a new level—and she would do it on her own terms. Over a glass of wine one evening, the new roommates got into a philosophical discussion about the perils of materialism and the merits of simplifying one's lifestyle. The conversation inspired them to act. Determined to break free from the shackles of materialism, the pair hatched a radical plan to go an entire year without purchasing anything. With a hasty toast to their new project, Buy Nothing Year was born.

For the next three months, they cut out all spending on material goods such as furniture, clothes, and housewares. Then, starting at the three-month mark, they stopped purchasing services like restaurant meals, coffees, haircuts, dry cleaning, and transportation (bus passes and gasoline). During the year, the only things they paid for were groceries, rent, and utilities, including their cell phones and internet. Everything else was either made by hand or eliminated from their lives completely. One exception was dish soap: after a few failed attempts at making it from scratch, they reluctantly had to purchase it from the store.

Buy Nothing Year was transformative for Julie. "I feel a greater depth, authenticity, and richness in my relationships. I have more clarity about my priorities and commitments. I feel more confident and clearer about what I want and who I am....It's infrequent these days for me to do something just because it's popular. I live by my own ethical code."

The more she peeled back the superficial layers of her life, the easier it was to see what really mattered to her. "In many ways," she said, "I felt like I was relearning values my parents instilled in me from childhood: qualities like self-reliance, resourcefulness, ingenuity, simplicity, and even shrewdness. The project felt like a process of remembering things I already knew but had somehow forgotten."

Julie's radical experiment helped her to uncover her core values, which were smothered under a mountain of material goods. Going cold turkey on consumerism is not for everyone; however, it's fair to say that most of us could benefit from scaling back at least a little bit. Adopting a more minimalist mindset is a good way to save money; and it also promotes a healthier, more balanced, self-sufficient lifestyle. Perhaps most important, shedding the materialistic layers of your life can reveal the bedrock of your values.

I experienced this when I transitioned from consulting to higher education. The move forced me to take a long, hard look at my personal finances and some of my lifestyle choices. I sold the convertible, cut back on pricey restaurant meals and entertainment expenditures, and slashed several other frivolous activities. With fewer distractions in my life, I had a lot more time to pursue things that brought me genuine fulfillment—which were, of course, the things that aligned with my core values.

My work at the university was fun and creative, provided opportunities for growth and development, and allowed me to make a difference in my students' lives. It was more rewarding and less stressful than my corporate job, and it didn't consume so much of my life. True, I didn't make as much money, but I felt greater contentment and had more time for side projects, recreation, reading, relationships, and travel. My life was much fuller.

Loss can simplify our lives for us because it leaves us little choice. But it's not the only way. We can be active in letting go of what's not important. By choosing to give up certain things that we don't really need, our true values will begin showing up. Plus, we'll have more time, room, and energy to connect with what does really matter.

LOOK TO YOUR PEAK EXPERIENCES

Masa Takei, a freelance writer from Vancouver, taught me that sometimes, you discover what really matters by looking *up*. By this, I mean paying attention to your "peak experiences."

We've probably all dreamed of trading in the daily grind of city living for a simpler, more tranquil lifestyle somewhere in the countryside. Anyone who has been on the nine-to-five treadmill long enough can probably relate to this brand of fantasy. In the spring of 2011, Masa did just that. He left his busy life in the city with a single purpose: to travel to Haida Gwaii, a remote 155-mile-long archipelago off the north coast of British Columbia nestled below the Alaska Panhandle, to build a small cabin and live off-the-grid for a whole year.

I asked Masa what compels a self-described "average urban guy" to trade his comfy existence for the rugged life on some faraway island.

"At some point, I had this realization that I'd managed to live almost four decades without ever physically building anything, let alone the shelter that I lived in. I'd never grown, gathered, or harvested the food that I ate, beyond the odd fish and handful of berries." While working in abstractions, shuffling symbols across a screen, he'd done nothing concrete to keep himself warm, dry, and fed. "So, I started with peeling the price tags off my tools and went from there."

He described his one-year experiment, which turned into two-and-a-half years, as a time filled with challenges and triumphs: the moment he declared his cabin complete, the time he surfed his first overhead wave, the day he walked out the front door with a rifle and returned home carrying a deer on his back. When I asked him about the big life lessons he learned from living off-the-grid, his answer surprised me.

"That question could fill a book," he said. "The short answer is that I thought the experience would be about learning self-sufficiency; instead, I learned the real importance of community.

"One day, in the midst of working on my cabin, I heard and then saw the fire engine from town go past with its siren on. There's only one road and fewer than a dozen residents on that part of the gravel road where I was living. If the fire truck was passing me, then it had to be a neighbor."

Masa jumped in his truck and found the brigade parked outside his good friend's cabin at the end of the road. The single mother who owned it was off the island, but within moments, other neighbors arrived to help. After the volunteer fire fighters hacked the roof apart and dowsed the smoldering hole, Masa and the others worked together to assemble a temporary patch on the roof to ensure no further damage from the elements would occur before the owner returned.

"I remember it like it was yesterday," Masa recalled. "In that moment, I realized how much I valued being part of this tightly knit group—part of something larger than myself."

This is the story that stands out the most for Masa when he recalls his time on Haida Gwaii. He thought he was seeking self-sufficiency and found community instead. This was his peak experience, and it allowed him the opportunity to reevaluate his core values.

We all have peak experiences from our own lives that can offer us this same opportunity. Yours shouldn't be too difficult to conjure up; in fact, they should stand out in your memory like prominent blips on a radar display. They are those defining moments when you felt most alive and aligned with who you really are.

Peak experiences can serve as beacons. Pay attention to these moments and ask yourself why they are important and memorable. Your answers can point the way to your most cherished values—and you might be surprised by what you discover.

WHAT WOULD INDY DO?

The third method I discovered for uncovering one's core values came from a little travel game (or habit) that I picked up over the years. I've already shared that Indiana Jones was my boyhood idol, so I like to think of myself as a mild-mannered version of Indy when I travel. Indy personifies adventure and boldness—two qualities that I hold in high regard. When abroad, I'm not searching for postcard-perfect beaches, drinking at glitzy hotel bars flooded with foreigners, or watching well-orchestrated cultural performances staged for tourists. Paradise for me is discovering a ruined temple while trekking through the jungle, snorkeling with sea turtles, or summiting a volcano at sunrise. So, when I am presented with a choice of how to spend my time, I often ask myself, *What would Indy do?*

This practice served me well when, during my time in Bali, a local friend that I'd made asked, "Do you want to attend a public cremation ceremony on Friday?"

I had trepidation. This was a new one for me. What would it entail? Gory sights I simply shouldn't witness? Would I be interloping on an intimate cultural ritual? I didn't know the answers to these questions, but I did know the answer to the question that mattered: What would Indy do? Deeply honored by the invitation and spurred on by my internal adventurer, I knew that neither I nor Indiana Jones would turn down this unusual opportunity.

To prepare, I educated myself on what to expect. I learned that in Balinese Hindu culture, cremation is an important rite of passage in the cycle of life, as it's believed to release the soul from the body so it can reincarnate. These ceremonies happen some months after a person's passing, or even years. After death, the body is buried for a period, then exhumed for cremation on the same day as other villagers. It's a communal affair. Bones from the deceased are placed in sarcophagi shaped like mythical animals and then burned after a long, high-spirited procession in a riot of colorful and rousing traditional music.

When we arrived at the ceremony, I was one of many people in the crowd—some participating, many witnessing, all connected. What impacted me the most was the gift of being invited into this community and the collective joyfulness of the occasion. Once again, following the instincts of my truest self (and Indiana Jones) had not let me down. Of course, I'm no Harrison Ford, and I'm not on a life-threatening quest for a lost artifact, but thinking like Indy helps to align my decisions with my values.

All experiences in life are more satisfying when they're tightly linked to your sense of who you are, or who you want to be. When plumbing for your values, you can learn a lot about yourself by taking a look at the people you emulate in life—from Gandhi to Indy, in my case—and taking stock of what it is about them that calls to you. Often, they represent an idealized version of yourself and your own values.

Whether you fashion yourself after Lara Croft, Amelia Earhart, or Bruce Lee, you'll be happier if you do things that align with your sense of self, even if it's an aspirational version of you. And remember, aspiring to be more in alignment with people you admire does not mean trying to be someone you're not; it's a version of you that personifies your most deeply held values and principles.

Your Compass for a Better Life

Whether you discover your core values through practicing simplicity, noticing peak experiences, or asking yourself what your alter ego would do (or, more likely, a combination of all three approaches), the point is this: Your values are your compass.

This compass will guide your actions, decisions, and interactions with others. By grounding yourself in your values, all areas of your life—from work and family to friendships, leisure, health, service, and spirituality—will feel interconnected and aligned. When your day-to-day behaviors are consistent with your values, you will feel greater peace, happiness, and fulfillment. It's a tremendously powerful way to live.

Through practicing these three methods to discover my values, I was able to create a list of the ten core qualities that resonate most with me at this stage of my life. Then I added a short phrase using active language to each one, to help me visualize what it would look like to put these values into practice. I came up with the following:

1. Adventure: Be open to new opportunities.

2. Boldness: Think big and take risks.

3. Community: Connect with others.

4. Contribution: Make the world a better place.

5. Creativity: Bring new ideas to life.

6. Fun: Enjoy myself and my work.

7. Growth: Develop and expand my mindset, knowledge, and abilities.

8. Integrity: Be true to my word and walk the talk.

9. Leadership: Lead by example—engage and empower others.

10. Respect: Show consideration for people and the planet.

In the exercises at the end of this week's chapter, you will be invited to begin creating your own list. Your values will be different from mine, and that's okay; they're highly personal. The important thing is that you believe in them. They should be what you aspire to and should paint a portrait of the person you want to be in the world.

With this in mind, you will begin approaching life with greater intention and striving every day to act in ways that are consistent with your

authentic self. This means consciously focusing on things that are significant to you while deliberately passing up the distractions.

Every day, you make a host of small decisions about how to allocate
your time, energy, and money. For example, let's say you get off work early
and have a few unplanned hours; how should you spend them? These
kinds of decisions might seem trivial in the moment, but given that you
make so many of them, their cumulative effect over months and years has
a huge impact on your life.

Making the most of your time doesn't mean you have to strive for the
profound and lofty. After all, this is not all Gandhi, all the time—this is
the Gandhiana Jones Project. Fun itself is a viable value. It's one of mine.
When I find myself with some spare time, I have a multitude of choices
that align with my list, but right off the top of my head, I might throw
together a picnic and go explore a new hiking trail or check out a new local
band. Whatever tops your list, being in alignment with your values is what
to strive for.

I know that if I stay true to my values more days than not, I will be the type
of person I like, respect, and can be proud of—and one my father would
have been proud of, too. My dad taught me many things, especially how to
live with integrity based on a set of higher principles. I know that in years
to come, my memory of him will be a constant presence in my life, gently
guiding me to stay true to my own values as I journey through this grand
adventure. Staying the course will be a tribute to his legacy, and my values
are the compass that will keep me on the path.

Week 1 Lesson Summary

- Trust your gut. If it keeps rumbling, that's a good indication that
  some aspect of your life is incompatible with your values, and it
  might be time to change direction.
- To uncover your values, try scaling back on some of the material

things in your life. Peeling away these superficial layers can give you a clearer view of what matters to you. Focus your energy there.

- Peak experiences can serve as markers for when you were living in alignment with your values. Ask yourself why these moments were important and memorable to you; your answers can point the way toward your values.

- The people and characters you emulate hold clues to your own values. When faced with a decision, you can ask yourself, *What would they do?* to align your own choices with those values.

- Once you know your values, you can use them to guide your actions, decisions, and interactions with others. Slowly but surely, these behaviors will form new habits that will shape your character into the best version of you.

Week 1 Exercises

Grab a pen and paper now while the information's still fresh, and if you're ready, start on these first exercises. Writing on a tablet or phone is okay, but using more traditional tools taps into an area of your brain that solidifies learning in a different way. If you're not ready to start now, other good times to do this work are at the end of the day or when you get up in the morning. Each exercise should take around fifteen minutes or so, but be flexible with yourself.

1. GUT CHECK

If you're having trouble identifying your values, then this exercise will be especially helpful. Are there any areas of your life where you are spending time doing things that don't feel good, or right, to you? Are there areas of discomfort? Think about all aspects of your life: work, recreation, relationships, health, finances, etc. Make a quick list of anything that comes to mind, from the big to the small.

Now, pick one thing from your list and answer the following questions: How long has this been going on? What was the sequence of events that led to this moment? Do you feel your principles are being compromised? If so, which ones? What is one small step you could take to bring this moment more in line with them?

2. LESS IS MORE

There is no doubt that stripping away the layers of materialism in your life can help reveal deeper values. A whole Buy Nothing Year is long and involved, but as a thought exercise, try this: Imagine you were barred from buying stuff, except for food and other necessities. What would you choose to do? What would you want to make for yourself? Why? You may find your answers quite revealing. Make a note of what values arise for you in this exercise.

3. PEAK EXPERIENCES

Identify one or two peak experiences from your past. To do this, think about events and moments when you felt really happy, fulfilled, and alive. What was special about these times? What emotions were you feeling? What characteristics or qualities were you exhibiting? What values are associated with these experiences?

4. WHAT WOULD YOUR ROLE MODEL DO?

List three people, real or fictional, whom you admire or aspire to be like. Try for a diverse range of sources, like Gandhi and Indiana Jones. What inspires you about them? What qualities do they display that you would like to cultivate in your own life? Brainstorm at least one action that you could take this week to emulate each person or character.

Now, pick one of them and practice asking yourself, "What would they do?" whenever you are faced with a decision this week.

5. NAME YOUR VALUES

You should now have a few values identified from the above exercises. Jot them all down together in one list. If there are any core values that you know are missing, add them to your list.

There is no magic number, but for this exercise, try to find ten if you can. Avoid the temptation to embrace values that look good on paper but don't reflect the real you. Sure, it would be impressive if I could grow my own food, rebuild an engine, or tile the bathroom floor, but in truth, being able to do those things is not that important to me. Even though I think self-sufficiency is an admirable quality in others, it does not appear on my list of values. Be honest with your own assessment. The more authentic you are in honoring your true values, the closer you will come to living your best life.

Once you have your selection, list them alphabetically: e.g., accountability, balance, curiosity, decisiveness, empathy, etc. This list represents what's important to you at this moment in your life, and it may shift later.

(If you're struggling to come up with ten values, you can find lists of this kind on the internet. Refer to the Notes section at the end of the book for some additional resources.)

6. VALUES IN ACTION

Using active language, write a short phrase to describe each of your values. For example, I define community as "connecting with others," and creativity as "bringing new ideas to life." This will help you visualize what's important to you and then put it into practice.

Weekly Challenge: Live Your Values

This week's challenge is to spend at least thirty minutes each day doing activities that are aligned with your values.

Now that you've uncovered your own values, it's time to put them into action. For each value on your list, jot down two or three activities that bring it to life. For example, if you value family, then your list may look like this:

- Send a handwritten card to someone in my family who could use encouragement.
- Plan a build-your-own pizza and ice-cream-sundae night where everyone gets to participate.
- Go bike riding with my nephew.

Maybe you value spontaneity:

- Try something new on a whim.
- Say yes to the next suggestion/request a friend makes.
- Strike up a spontaneous conversation with a stranger.

In some cases, an activity might involve more than one value; for example, taking part in a flash mob would embrace my values for adventure and community.

Now, go out and do some of these things! You don't have to do all the activities that you dream up, but do make sure to touch upon all your values this week and see how they fit.

Finally, don't forget to journal about your experiences with this weekly challenge before moving on to Week 2. It's an important tool for maximizing learning and to help make new behaviors stick. For more direction, refer to the guide for self-reflection in the Appendix.

WEEK 2

PASSION: FUELING UP FOR THE JOURNEY

In doing something, do it with love or never do it at all.
– MAHATMA GANDHI

Indiana Jones: What do you do for money?

Mutt Williams: Fix motorcycles...you got a problem with that?

Indiana Jones: Not if that's what you love doing.
Don't let anybody tell you different.*

"DO YOU LIKE MOSQUITOES?" DR. FROG ASKED IN A FAUX-FRENCH accent, wiggling his bright-red clown's nose as he spoke.

The seven-year-old boy across from him sat up in bed, a look of feigned suspicion on his face. "Not really," said the young patient, eyebrows furrowed. "Why do you ask?"

*Indiana Jones and the Kingdom of the Crystal Skull (2008)

"We're having a mesquite-o barbecue later," the doctor deadpanned, bursting into a huge smile a moment later as the child broke out in giggles. From there, the doctor moseyed on down the hallway of St. Justine's Children's Hospital, looking to inject another dose of lighthearted humor into the next person he met.

Dr. Frog, dressed like a cowboy physician in his white coat, checked shirt, blue jeans, scuffed Stetson hat, and boots, is also known as Alexis Roy. He's a member of the Dr Clown Foundation, a nonprofit organization in Montreal, Canada. Roy and other specially trained clowns work in hospitals, care homes, and other institutions to bring cheer to an atmosphere that's normally anything but funny. The moments of levity he provides improve the quality of life for staff, patients, and families alike.

I met with one of the organization's founders, Melissa Holland. Countless studies, she told me, corroborated years of experiential evidence showing the health benefits of laughter and humor. Physiological effects include cascades of endorphins and other natural chemicals in the body that reduce stress and pain, while emotional effects include strengthened social bonds and increased resilience to trauma; naturally, clowns facilitate all these states. "Think Charlie Chaplin...or Mr. Bean," she enthused. "The clown's tools are his body and his emotions. Through them, he is able to express anger, sadness, happiness, fear, relief, and disappointment."

Melissa was obviously passionate about this topic, and I asked her how this connected with her journey in her career. She told me that as a theater student in college, she'd loved acting but felt that something was missing: service, a strong value she had grown up with. With this realization, she'd enrolled in a program called Arts in Human Development at Concordia University in Montreal. The focus on working with vulnerable populations was a good fit for her. Next came a series of clowning workshops. With each piece of learning, she was able to explore many different outlets for her multiple passions. "Ultimately, clowning was the most creative, profound, spiritual work I had ever done," Melissa told me, beaming. "But then I closed the door on that passion, thinking that I would never use it in my life because I didn't want to be a party or circus clown."

Melissa moved to Scotland and started teaching high school drama, but she found it unrewarding. She came across a magazine ad recruiting people to work as "clown doctors" in pediatric healthcare settings. Intrigued at what sounded like an opportunity to combine her passion and qualifications, she applied and was hired. "I could be silly, stupid, vulnerable, and make sick children laugh—and get paid for it," she told me.

Rocket-propelled by her passion, Melissa never looked back.

When she returned home to Canada, she connected with a few others who shared her values and love for clowning, and within a year, they'd started a therapeutic clown program in Montreal out of the Montreal Children's Hospital. The Dr Clown Foundation was born.

Today, the foundation serves more than seventy facilities in the province of Quebec and boasts a team of over fifty professional clown doctors from a variety of backgrounds, including the performing arts, education, psychology, and medicine. Between 2015 and 2020, the foundation doubled in size and scope, expanding into working with adults in palliative care as well as children with a wide variety of needs, including those on the autism spectrum, those with physical and intellectual disabilities, kids with mental health issues, and those in foster care. They have also started a school to both train new clown doctors and educate healthcare workers.

Passion provided the initial spark of interest that started Melissa down her path, but it's also the fuel that has kept her going over all these years. This is the reward for pursuing passion-driven work. It generates its own positive feedback loop; as you continue to reinject yourself with energy, you'll boost your motivation and keep working toward your goal. Joy and contentment will arise naturally out of this wholehearted immersion in your work.

And there's more good news. Identifying your passions isn't nearly so complex as uncovering your values. All it takes is curiosity, play, authenticity, and some commitment.

Ready to start?

Discovering Your Passions

During my twenties, whenever someone queried about my passions, I'd reply vaguely with something like, "Oh, I'm really into some deep theoretical stuff right now," hoping to sound impressive. I never had a genuine answer to this question because, in all honesty, I didn't feel like I had a true passion. There was nothing I felt compelled to do. Under the mistaken assumption that everyone comes hardwired with things they love in life, I thought there might be something wrong with me. There wasn't.

In our youth, we're still figuring a lot out. We shouldn't expect to know our passions (and parents should not expect this of their children, either). Sure, some of us are clear early in life about what lights us up, and we stick with these pursuits through thick and thin. But the rest of us will likely experiment with options, testing the waters and following our curiosity to see what feels good, then spend time gradually nurturing those things. After a while, if our attraction has grown, we can continue learning and exploring; and with time, a deeper passion might bloom. Or if it has faded, we can simply move on to the next thing that piques our interest.

When I was a kid, my parents took me to a figure-skating show where skaters in massive costumes performed a choreographed routine on ice—but what really captured my attention was the drummer in the supporting band. Once home, I begged my parents to enroll me in drum lessons for weeks, until they relented. I stuck with it for a year but could never replicate that sound from the show, so I gave up. I say this not because I think I should have kept at it; I don't regret my dabbling, as it was all part of the process.

In childhood, we're often encouraged to pursue what we're good at, especially in school. But we aren't necessarily passionate about these things. The reverse can also be true, in that we are not always good at the things we're passionate about, but we can work to improve. The point isn't to be the best, but to find fulfillment from doing things that bring us joy. It's normal and healthy to sample a large variety of interests before discovering a few that resonate authentically. It's a sign of an active mind—one that is open and explorative, not focused on failure or success. This is sometimes referred to as the "beginner's mind." As we'll see in Week 3, cultivating such openness to experimentation is not only valuable as a means to nurture possible passions, but also a way to develop new skills and abilities.

Most important, time spent following your curiosity through investigating and encouraging your interests provides space for passion to bloom.

Focus on Your Inner Child

If you are struggling to identify your latent passions, you actually have an inner storehouse that you can access: your childhood. Your early memories allow you to access a time when passion was a natural part of your everyday life.

When I was a young kid, I had a camera. It was a cheap, no-frills little plastic thing, but it actually worked. On family outings, I'd be our documentarian, snapping dozens of pictures of our clan. I had a lot of fun and received encouragement and compliments for my efforts, and I found it was a form of expression that came easily to me. As an adult, I bought a better-quality camera and pursued the hobby more intentionally by enrolling in photography classes. I really enjoyed getting familiar with some of the more technical aspects of the craft. Then other things in my life took precedence, and long stretches would elapse when I didn't go out to shoot.

At one point, I was packing for a two-week trip and found my camera equipment in the back of a closet. It had been gathering dust for over five years.

Oh, what a loss, I thought at first. *Why did I give that up?* But then, realizing the unkindness of my self-talk, I reframed the question. *Do I still love this?* This generated a new thought. *Okay, Joe, dust off your Nikon and put it in your suitcase. I challenge you to take just one photo a day on your trip. If you can do that, you get to keep the camera!*

I had a sense that the new surroundings on my trip would rekindle my interest. But I was also open to letting go of the camera if I didn't enjoy myself. What I didn't want was for it to remain in my closet, being of use to no one.

One of the stops during my trip was Boston. I remember waking up one morning, pining for caffeine. I glanced out the window, and the air was swirling with snowflakes. It appeared a minor blizzard was underway—a great day to take pictures! But first, I needed to get that coffee. Then, remembering my challenge, I realized this was the perfect opportunity to combine the two tasks.

I typed "best coffee shop in Boston" into my smartphone. Up sprang Polcari's Coffee on Salem Street, sporting a rare five-star rating. Eureka! I met up with a friend and off we went. Given the weather, I kept my phone safely in my pocket and out of the blowing snow as we zigzagged through the empty, icy streets for over an hour. We passed storefront windows, their glowing amber light beckoning us into the warmth, but we were on a mission. After dead ends and wrong turns, we finally arrived at our destination in the heart of the city's historic Italian neighborhood. Waltzing through the front door of the quaint shop, we were surprised to find not a single espresso machine on-site, but rather a vast assortment of coffee beans, tea, and spices, as well as pasta, deli meats, candy, and nuts.

Polcari's was a coffee *store*, not a coffee *shop*. Laughing at ourselves, we browsed the wares for a few minutes, then took off down the block to find a run-of-the-mill café. After we ordered, I took out my camera and snapped a photo from the doorway, looking down the narrow street lined with brownstone houses. One thing I love about this photo is how it picks up the light reflecting off the falling snowflakes. And of course, it still reminds me of that passionate wintry quest to find the perfect cappuccino and the perfect photo. May all my bungled adventures, both big and small, bring so much joy.

I did meet my challenge of shooting one photo a day on that trip. Not every shot was all that memorable, but I had fun every day following my instincts and finding interesting sights to capture. My challenge reignited a passion that I had forgotten to nurture. It provided a low-stress format to tune in to my inner child—the little guy who loved to take snapshots as a way of capturing special moments. And I tapped into something deeper, too: the fearless and fun way that I approached taking pictures as a kid.

I kept my camera and continued learning about the art form, creating more exciting photographic projects for myself and, later, for my students as well. Photography has remained an incredibly gratifying pursuit, but not just that; my renewed commitment to this passion led to opportunities for service and engagement with my community that I could never have imagined. I'll tell you more about that a bit later in the book.

Child's Play

Reviving our childhood passions can be a lot of fun, and it can also be revealing. You might just remember something long neglected that you love doing. However, your preferences may have changed significantly since childhood. What's most important is to revisit the state of mind of a child at play; we should embrace and cultivate it in our adult lives, too, as that open, creative, curious mindset nourishes us and allows our passion to grow.

If you struggle with invoking your own inner child, then how about seeking some guidance from an actual kid? I don't have children, so one afternoon, I took my friend's son on an excursion around my neighborhood. We didn't have a set plan or destination. I told him our mission was simply to have an adventure, then let his active five-year-old's imagination take the wheel. We explored alleyways, walked along an abandoned railway track, ran through a water fountain, played tag in a playground, and raced down the sidewalk in a junked stroller. It was one of the best days I'd had in a very long time. I borrowed a kid, but even if you have your own, I'd argue you could still carve out some time for deliberate open-ended play.

It's easy to get caught up in the hustle and bustle of our lives. We are task oriented, and there's a lot of pressure—both from the outside and within ourselves—to check off our to-do lists with efficiency. Rarely do we give ourselves permission to play, with no objective other than to enjoy the moment and experience the sensations that come from being immersed in it.

It's not the pursuit of excellence that drives children to play; their sandcastles are not scale replicas or flawless works of art, but they probably don't notice or care. They're too immersed in the moment—creating, uninhibited, with an open and inventive mind. Looking at the world through the eyes of a child can help remind us that life is, on some level, a great big playground. Having fun is not just a fringe benefit; it's key to living a passionate, productive life.

Fearless Authenticity

As young children, we don't need to be taught how to be ourselves. We just *are* ourselves. But once we're at school, we learn to conform. Standardized curricula and testing give us limited opportunities to explore what truly makes us feel alive, open, and curious. After years of being shaped and molded into productive test-takers and essay-writers, we may, by the time we reach college, be afraid to color outside the lines and express ourselves authentically. Passions may be buried or latent. And the fear of judgment from others (parents, teachers, friends, society) may stop us from exploring these things. Rather, we focus our time and energy on trying to meet external expectations—real or perceived.

Many of us build careers and live out our lives according to external influences and expectations, rather than following a more authentic path. What's ironic is that, as we get older, we come to admire and respect people who are true to themselves—individuals who are living passionate lives focused on what lights them up, whatever that may be. So, why not be that kind of person? What does it take?

It takes courage, for one, to follow your heart and be your authentic self in the world. Many of us have not been given the opportunity to practice doing this in a safe environment. Nor have we been taught how to deal with criticism (both from others and from ourselves, i.e., our inner critic). Those stifling critics can stop us before we even start.

Learning to be our true selves also means focusing on what we love. This is the domain of passion. The first assignment I gave my students in the Project Change course was designed to help them pay attention to what they love, and in doing so, to tap into their passions and discover new aspects of themselves.

In the exercise, each student was instructed to create a photo series illustrating an issue of relevance in their world. Knowing that young people are often swayed by their peer group, I encouraged them not to make choices based on anyone else, but to focus on what lights them up. If they weren't sure what that was, then they could choose something they were curious about, or even pick something new just for fun. The most important thing was that it felt genuine to them. At the end of the assignment, we took some time in class to view a selection of the photos, and students could then share more information about the issues. We even had an informal awards ceremony that recognized achievement in several categories: best technical, best photographs, best concept, most creative, most visual.

One year, a student named Thomas, who was an avid mountain biker, prepared his photo essay on the impacts of mountain biking on trails and mountains around Vancouver. His photographs were outstanding. In one, a trail cuts through the lush temperate rainforest. What stands out in the photo are the deep, exposed roots of the trees that border the trail, eroded from heavy traffic and the resulting increases in water runoff. I hadn't given much thought to the idea that biking (what I consider a healthy sport) could have such a destructive effect on the environment. This photo, along with the others in his series, brought this important issue to life. His submission earned an A-plus.

Shortly afterward, Thomas came to see me during my office hours.

He told me, choking up with emotion, that this was the first A he had ever received.

I later learned that he struggled with academics due to a learning disability, which made it challenging for him to perform in exams and other traditional assessments. It had undermined his confidence significantly.

This assignment had given him a chance to connect with what he deeply loves and share this part of himself with others. It was a moment I'll always remember and one of those occasions that makes you proud to be a teacher. I thought I could see a new sense of self-assurance in him as he grinned and turned to stride out of my office.

There are many voices in this world trying to persuade us to be like everyone else: to wear the same things, listen to the same music, live the same lifestyles. It can be hard to choose your own path and do your own thing. But if you can untether yourself from external influences and opinions and connect at heart-level with yourself, you will ignite a fire that burns hot and bright. This inner spark will drive you much more than external rewards and recognition can. This is passion-fueled, fearless authenticity, and it can change the world.

Commit to Your Passions

Living a life that's in alignment with your passions doesn't mean following every whim or giving up on your responsibilities and obligations; it means choosing something with potential and putting in the work to see it grow. Holman Wang sums up this concept this way: "Ride mule, chase horse." Allow me to explain.

During his childhood, Holman spent as much time as possible drawing, painting, and building models. Creativity was part of his identity and a true passion. A veritable Renaissance man at the age of thirty-eight, with degrees in law, education, and architectural history in his pocket, he had been practicing law for five years at a big downtown firm in Vancouver when he noticed that he was feeling disenchanted with the job. Holman had reservations about the legal profession: the emotional emptiness of the work, the reverence for money, and the never-ending stress. He wanted a change—one that would allow him to do something creative. Around this time, his twin brother, Jack (an author and college professor specializing in fiction writing), contacted him with an idea for a series of children's picture books. He wanted to work with Holman to make it happen. Although he was not a trained illustrator, the pull of creative possibilities made Holman jump at the opportunity.

The concept was simple: condense a classic novel down to twelve child-friendly words, with an illustration appearing alongside each one. The words are carefully selected to relate to a child's world, such as "sisters," "sick," and "no" for *Pride and Prejudice*, and "boat," "mad," and "whale" for *Moby Dick*. From this idea, the *Cozy Classics* series evolved. Jack abridges the text, and Holman creates the illustrations. The resulting books are delightfully original and wildly popular.

"I didn't think I could compete with professional children's book illustrators just by picking up a paintbrush, so I tried to think outside the box for a way to create the images," Holman told me. By watching YouTube videos and learning by trial and error, he learned the art of needle-felting. Through this process, which entails stabbing at loose wool fibers with a barbed needle, he created detailed three-dimensional figures, which he then photographed on sets and in locations outdoors.

The pair prepared a book proposal and sample pages, then sought a publishing deal, and before long, they landed one. The books began to take off; in 2012, with two published books and more on the drawing board, Holman resigned from the law firm to become a full-time children's book illustrator. With two young kids at home and bills to pay, this wasn't an inconsequential decision—it had to lead to a *successful* artistic career.

What appeared to the outside world to be an audacious career move was actually almost a seamless transition, because the foundation had already been built, so there were minimal risks. Holman's mindset was already primed as well.

This is where the Chinese proverb "Ride mule, chase horse" comes in. "I learned it from my parents," said Holman, "probably in my mid-twenties. It was their risk-averse advice for changing jobs. They weren't the go-for-it types. I've modified the lesson to spark larger life changes, but obviously I believe in the importance of laying a lot of groundwork for change."

The mule represents the stability you've already got, and the horse symbolizes the dream you're chasing. In other words, while nurturing your passions (the horse), don't give up your day job (the mule).

Making the jump from one to the other requires commitment. The "ride mule, chase horse" principle means you must work extra hard—which, according to Holman, might not be a bad thing. Your day job provides stable income. Giving that up suddenly can wreak havoc on your bank account and your self-esteem, so don't be quick to ditch it, despite the temptation. "Hang on to that job as long as you can," advises Holman, "but make room in your life for your true passion. This gives you a low-risk space to explore. If the alternative career takes off, you can go part-time or even quit your day job. If the alternative career doesn't materialize, you're not left destitute and directionless. Doubling down on your workload is career change the hard way, but for many people, it may be the only way."

Doubling down means pursuing your passion in your off-hours, at least until you can prove its financial viability. This is a good test: Are you willing to chip away at a side project on the weekends after spending all week "working for the man"? Holman was, because he loved making art. He had energy for it and required no outside motivation. It didn't come without sacrifice, however; he had to cut back on ordinary pleasures like watching TV, sleeping in, and nights out, but the enjoyment and fulfillment more than made up for it. If you're willing to make such a sacrifice without it feeling like a burden, then it's a good indication that passion is fueling this change.

Holman shows it's possible to take risks while still playing it smart, to explore a new career while maintaining your salary. The frustration you may feel in your current job can motivate you—if you don't fight your natural ebbs and flows of creativity. Holman suggests using the fallow periods to contemplate new ideas, acquire skills, and build up energy that you can unleash on the world later. For example, Holman learned about contracts in his job at the law firm. So, when he was offered a publishing contract for his books, he could read and understand it and negotiate the terms without needing to hire an agent or lawyer. Many skills are transferable. Even if you feel that your current career is unsatisfying, perhaps you can view it from a longer-term perspective and see that some of the things you're learning may help you on future projects that are aligned with your passions.

Holman also proves that it's possible to do more than one thing as a career; a few years into publishing, he went back to practicing law independently part-time, allowing him to set his own schedule and leave plenty of time for making books. This way of practicing law eliminated some of the issues he had working at a big firm, rekindled his interest for his original career, and brought in an additional source of income for his family. His story shows that it is possible to take risks while playing it safe. But more important, it reveals the rewards that are possible when one is willing to fully commit to pursuing a passion-fueled life.

Week 2 Lesson Summary

- While some of us may know what we love doing from an early age and pursue it throughout life, for most of us, passion will take gradual nurturing. With an open and curious mind, explore new things and pay attention to what excites you. Your interest may fade quickly or blossom into something more. When you discover your true passions, you will have found a fuel that can keep you motivated and energized for a lifetime.
- Look to your childhood memories for passions you may have forgotten. Your early memories allow you to access a time when passion was a natural part of your everyday life.

- Cultivate the state of mind of a child at play. It is this type of open, creative, curious mindset that allows passion to develop.

- Don't follow the crowd or others' advice—especially if you haven't asked for it—unless it feels right to you. There is no reason to be overly concerned about what other people may think about what you do. Be fearless in following your authentic path.

- While nurturing your passions (the horse), don't give up your day job (the mule). And remember, you may need to ride that mule for a long time before you catch that horse. Following your passions requires total commitment to your dream—but if you are on the right track, passion will also be the fuel that powers this journey.

Week 2 Exercises

1. FOLLOW YOUR CURIOSITY

Just like you did with values last week, you are going to identify and create a list of your personal passions. The best place to start when plumbing for passions is to look to your own curiosity. Jot down some things that pique your interest in different areas—for example, intellectual pursuits, art, music, nature, health and fitness, recreation, relationships, etc. Now, take it to the next level. In conversations with friends, what lights you up, gets you excited, and gives you energy? What do you spend time reading about, watching, or listening to? Are you an expert on a certain topic or field of study? Use your answers to start assembling your list of passions.

2. LOOK TO YOUR CHILDHOOD

Think back to times in your childhood when you were creative, happy, playful, and open. List five things that you enjoyed doing. Now ask yourself: What activities could I do now to experience that kind of joy? Use your answers to continue building your list of passions.

3. NO REGRETS

What would you do with your life if you had no fears and no need to please others? Imagine being near the end of that life and looking back with no regrets. What are the top three things you are (or would be) proud to have done or tried? Spend some time in written exploration.

4. ARE YOU READY TO COMMIT?

If you currently have a passion project on the go, or are pursuing specific interests more deeply, here are some questions to contemplate—there are no wrong answers:

Can you imagine being happily engaged in your current favorite activity several decades from now? If you knew it would take you 10,000 more hours to master your best skill, would you keep working at it? Do you have FOMO (fear of missing out)? (Some of us are reluctant to commit to things because we worry we'll miss other opportunities. Remember, there will always be more.) Would you be willing to give up other things in order to succeed in this endeavor?

Weekly Challenge: Nurture Your Passions

For this week's challenge, you will be spending at least thirty minutes daily doing something that brings you joy—emphasis on the word *doing*.

That's right! This week is going to be full of joyful activities. Drawing from your newly minted list of passions, brainstorm some activities that will allow you to engage with what you love.

If music is on your list, don't just listen to music or watch an online concert—go ahead and make music. It doesn't matter how: with your voice, with an instrument if you have one, or you could just play drums with a few plastic containers and kitchen tools, like a kid would.

If it's a sport that lights you up, get a game together with friends.

Hone your skills by watching a video online and then practicing in your backyard.

Perhaps you love cheese; you could try out some new recipes, or even take a cheesemaking class. However crazy it seems, give it a try. You may feel a little nervous or silly, but I bet you will also feel excited, inspired, and energized.

Just a little note: For some of you, this might be easy, while for others, you may have to quell that voice inside telling you to "get to work." This will be work in its own way, but once you manage to let go and follow your inner child around a bit, it just might change your life.

Once again, don't forget to journal about your experiences with this weekly challenge before moving on to Week 3. For more direction, refer to the guide for self-reflection in the Appendix.

WEEK 3

SKILLS:
STOCKING YOUR TOOLKIT

**Live as if you were to die tomorrow. Learn
as if you were to live forever.**
– MAHATMA GANDHI

Lao Che: You never told me you spoke
my language, Doctor Jones.

Indiana Jones: Only on special occasions.*

MATT CARTER SAT ACROSS THE TABLE FROM ME IN A SMALL,
bustling café. His affable manner broke the ice immediately, and within
minutes, we were reminiscing about our favorite bands from the 1990s.
For some, this era was marked by groups that dominated the radio
charts, like Aerosmith or Oasis, but not for Matt. Punk and the underground scene rocked his world.

*Indiana Jones and the Temple of Doom (1984)

"I loved the vibe and energy," Matt told me. And as a creative person (a musician, photographer, and writer), he felt he had something to contribute as more than just a spectator. Back in the mid-1990s, he reached out—in what he calls an "I-can-do-this moment"—to event organizers in his town of Fredericton, seeking an apprenticeship opportunity. With time and hard work, he learned the ropes of the business. Eventually, he rented his own warehouse space, and went on to host some of the biggest alternative acts in Canada at the time.

Fast-forward a few more years, and Matt had branched off into marketing and management in the mainstream arts community. He still pursued his own creative work in his spare time, but he felt disconnected from the underground music scene. At this time, alternative acts were fighting to get any media coverage at all. The city's free weekly arts-and-entertainment paper had recently stopped publication, so Matt, in another I-can-do-this moment, seized the opportunity; he launched his own online magazine, and today, *Grid City Magazine* is still giving local artists a voice, with event listings, interviews, photo essays, videos, and more.

While we sipped our coffee, Matt shared the most important lesson he had learned over the years. "Embrace what you do well. Everyone has something unique they bring to the table."

For Matt, his "something" was a combination of his love for music, innate resourcefulness, and the project management and communication skills he had learned. There are any number of projects that Matt could have pursued, but ultimately, what counted was that he found a way to align his skills with his values and passions. And he wasn't afraid to go out and learn new skills as needed. This is the sweet spot, where a rewarding life meets positive impact in the community.

What's in Your Toolkit?

I've talked about passion as the fuel for your journey—but it's not enough on its own. You're also going to need a toolkit as you equip yourself for the road ahead. This toolkit is made up of your skills.

Before setting off on any journey, you must take inventory of your gear to determine what you have, what you need to add, and what others might contribute, too. All these things should be part of your toolkit.

Let's say that you, like Matt Carter, love music and want to share it with the world. What tools and skills will you need? Perhaps you can sing or play an instrument. You may also have a strong understanding of music theory or history, and that's great. But you don't need to actually be a musician if you don't possess those skills or wish to learn them.

Aside from music-related tools, what else might be in your kit? Perhaps you have web design experience and could start a fan site for your favorite band. Maybe you're deft at bringing people together and could organize a fundraising concert for an important cause—or, if you're a talented writer, pen an article about local musicians. By applying your abilities to something you care about, you'll be well on your way to a life that is both rewarding and impactful.

When taking stock of the skills you already possess, remember that knowledge and skills are two sides of the same coin. Knowledge provides the foundation from which new ideas spring, and skills let you put them into practice. Both are required to make a meaningful contribution. Thinking back to Indiana Jones: he possesses deep knowledge of ancient civilizations, can speak dozens of languages, and knows how to wield a bullwhip. All are important assets on his adventures.

Once you've taken stock of what skills you possess and how you may develop them further, don't stop there. Consider what other skills you may need, and then get busy adding them to your toolkit as well. This may seem daunting, but with the right mindset, you can set yourself up for success.

Think Like a Beginner

Over the course of my career, I've accumulated a great deal of skills and knowledge for my toolkit, including project management, research, and presentation skills. But that doesn't mean there isn't room for more. One of the greatest delights of life is the opportunity to learn, and one can never be so accomplished that there is nothing left to discover.

At certain times in my life, I seek out specific skills to assist me with a project I am working on, just as Matt did when seeking out an apprenticeship. Other times, I simply seek out new skills for the joy of it, not knowing exactly how or where I might apply them but certain they will benefit me in some way.

As we learned in Week 2, childhood passions are a great source of inspiration. As a kid, I enjoyed drawing, so I thought it would be fun to revisit the subject as an adult. After searching online, I registered for a beginner drawing class at a nearby school. At our first session, I joined the dozen other adult learners in a big room, a pencil and stack of white paper in front of me on an easel. The instructor set up various objects at the front of the classroom and then told us to draw what we saw.

I was puzzled. The instructor hadn't shown us how to do anything, and I hadn't drawn anything since elementary school. How should I start? With a line? A dot? Should I sketch out the whole scene in front of me, or just start in one corner? My confusion morphed into frustration. *Hey,* I thought, *I'm paying to learn, and she isn't teaching.* The instructor said nothing helpful during the entire three-hour stretch. I went home disappointed, with several sheets of half-hearted scribbles.

Determined to have a different experience the next week, I raised my hand as soon as the instructor gave us the very same exercise. "Could you give us some basic tips?" I asked.

"What do you want to know exactly?" she replied.

Tamping down my growing impatience, I replied, "Well, for one, how should I hold the pencil?"

It turns out that for drawing lines and curves, it's better to invert the pencil in your hand and hold it more like a ping-pong paddle. I wasn't alone in my ignorance of this fact.

For the rest of the course, the teacher was no more forthcoming with instruction, and I would occasionally ask for some guidance—but less and less so as the course progressed, because the experience began to change for me. I had gone into the class expecting to learn key theories, concepts, and techniques that would help me improve. In other words, I wanted to learn the "rules" of art, and I wanted a sense of measurable progress. I had forgotten why I had signed up in the first place: to reengage with something I liked when I was a kid. But I wasn't thinking like a child—I was thinking like an adult. And I certainly wasn't thinking like a beginner. Once I realized this, I was able to let go of my expectations and enjoy myself.

What I didn't know then was that, in the moment I embraced a beginner's mindset, I was learning an entirely new skill: how to move from analytical to creative thought. This would serve me for the rest of my life.

I often turn to drawing now when I'm brainstorming. Not because I'm good at it—I'm not. However, I am freer when drawing than I am when writing to express new ideas and think outside the box, without the constant interruptions of a well-meaning yet stifling inner critic. I have also incorporated drawing into the classroom, where it has proven very useful with my students for brainstorming and doing visioning activities.

Approaching new things with the eye of a beginner allows you to broaden your horizons. Exploration, not perfection, should be your aim. Just like training for a sport, it's the learning that is important, not the finished product. Some people call this being "process-oriented" as opposed to "goal-oriented." I don't think they're mutually exclusive, but process orientation can ensure that you enjoy yourself along the way to accomplishing your goals.

Nurture a Growth Mindset

Manute Bol and Muggsy Bogues are both stars in the US National Basketball Association (NBA). Both had successful careers that spanned over a decade, which is more than twice the average length of an NBA career. They even played on the same team, the Washington Bullets, for one year in 1987. Looking at them, you might be forgiven for assuming that's where their similarities end.

At 7'7", Manute Bol is one of the tallest players in the league's history. He came by his height honestly, with his mother at 6'10" and his dad at 6'8". Their ethnic group—the Dinka people of South Sudan—are widely considered to be some of the tallest people in Africa, but even among them, Bol's family was above average. Manute came to basketball relatively late (he was fifteen when he started playing), but no one was particularly surprised that a fellow of his stature would excel at the sport.

On the other hand, Muggsy Bogues, at 5'3", is the shortest player ever to play in the NBA. He was born in Baltimore, Maryland, and grew up in the housing projects, raised by his mother after his father went to prison.

In a stroke of marketing genius, these two outliers at either end of the height spectrum were placed side-by-side for a Bullets promotional poster during their year as teammates. The staggering twenty-eight-inch height difference gave new meaning to the phrase "navel gazing," as Muggsy is barely taller than the waistline of Manute's shorts, while Manute's white-striped knee socks come up to Muggsy's hips.

In a game where height is such an important asset, it might be tempting to assume that the sky-high Manute Bol outscored the pocket-sized Muggsy Bogues. But that's not what happened; Muggsy scored a total of 6,858 points throughout his NBA career, compared to 1,599 points for Manute. Incredible. The shortest player ever in the history of the NBA scored over five thousand more points than one of the tallest players! How is this possible?

What Muggsy Bogues lacked in height, he made up for in speed on the floor. Weaving around taller defenders, he advanced the basketball up and down the court, keeping it safe and opening up scoring opportunities for himself and his teammates. He also had a strong growth mindset. Muggsy refused to simply accept the conventional standards that he was too short to play basketball. In fact, in interviews he's said his height—or lack thereof—was an advantage.

When it comes to learning and eventually mastering a new skill, your mindset matters—a lot. Stanford University psychologist Carol Dweck has conducted decades of research on the critical role of mindsets in achievement and success. In her book *Mindset*, Dweck details two different attitudes people hold about abilities and how these can affect personal development.

The first is a Fixed Mindset. With this way of thinking, one's abilities are as predetermined as our physical attributes: blue eyes, an ability to play basketball—they're the same. People are just born with talents, like sports, math, music, etc. If you're lucky, you can reap the benefits of natural talent, but if not, there's no point in trying. Any setbacks when trying to learn a new skill will reinforce this belief, causing you to give up when faced with the slightest obstacle or avoid challenges altogether. Unsurprisingly, this is not a recipe for success.

The second mindset is what Dweck calls a Growth Mindset. Individuals with a growth mindset believe that abilities and talents can be developed through focus, time, and energy. Practice is highly valued because it leads to improvement. Setbacks are not internalized as proof of lack of talent but viewed as integral to the process and key to building resilience. Most high achievers think this way.

In his book *Outliers*, Malcolm Gladwell examines a range of people who have achieved mastery of a skill set. He found that, across different disciplines, it takes approximately ten thousand hours of practicing a skill to truly master it. To quote Gladwell, "Practice isn't the thing you do once you're good. It's the thing you do that makes you good."

Not all practice is the same, however. Differences in performance tend to be affected by how much a person engages in *deliberate practice*, which involves breaking down a skill into its basic components, then methodically and repetitively performing activities to improve each. It's not until you become proficient at the individual components that you can put them all together to develop more complex skills. Deliberate practice is not a magic bullet; it requires time, patience, discipline, and determination. But if you can muster all these things, you will reap the rewards.

Experience Is the Best Teacher

Throughout your life journey, you'll want to keep honing your skills, whether you're just out of the starting gate or an expert in your field. There is nothing quite like getting started on a project to shed light on any additional skills you need to get the job done.

Like many university instructors, I was hired for my subject expertise, not my teaching ability. I thought teaching would come easily, that I'd glide into class and effortlessly dazzle the students with all my knowledge. Instead, I bored them with long-winded lectures delivered from a podium. Eventually, the sea of blank, apathetic faces and empty seats got to me. Once my bruised ego recovered, I got busy acquiring the skills I needed to do my job. I enrolled in a program that taught teachers how to teach and quickly learned why my first trials in the classroom had flopped; I'd envisioned myself as a wise old sage, transferring his knowledge to his pupils from the podium at the front of the room. In pedagogical terms, this is an instructor-centered approach to teaching, which doesn't help students learn to think for themselves. For my students to get the most out of my classes and succeed to graduation and beyond, I needed to shift my approach and bring their classroom experience and needs to the center.

Back in front of my own class and equipped with my new skills, I put into action what I'd learned. Every week, I would get up in front of the class—refining and testing, observing what my students responded to, and asking for feedback until I found what worked. Over time, I was able to use my classroom experience to refine the skills I had been taught. And my hard work paid off, as evidenced by the engaged looks on my students' faces, as well as my own sense of deep gratification for my work.

CONSIDER COACHING

We can all benefit from our own experience by learning from our missteps and correcting our course as we go along. But what if you're missing a key competency or the confidence needed to achieve your goals? You can look to someone else's experience. I'd venture to say that most people who reach the top have had a hand up along the way.

Coaching is one of the fastest-growing fields today, and for good reason; there are numerous ways to benefit from this form of hands-on skills transference. There are companies that provide coaching services in many different fields, and individuals who share their knowledge and skills on a professional basis. It's also easy to search for and access coaching options online.

When it comes to selecting a coach, fit is everything. Make sure to do some research about your prospective coaches, their experience, and their accreditation. Coaches do not necessarily need to have experience in your area and may be gifted at guiding you every step of the way simply because they are highly skilled at motivating. Consider what kind of coaching would benefit you most.

Most coaches charge a fee, so if this is a barrier for you, consider peer coaching, which doesn't involve any financial cost. It's an excellent way to develop skills and also promotes collaboration and community-building among your colleagues. I have used peer coaching from experts to target specific areas for improvement, and I found focusing on one specific skill at a time more manageable than receiving feedback about my entire performance.

Whether you pursue paid or peer options, coaching can accelerate the learning and development process by:

- assisting you with defining goals and the steps to achieving them
- giving one-on-one feedback and support for improving specific skills
- providing a safe environment to develop skills, which allows for deeper learning and higher levels of comfort with the skill
- helping to build personal awareness (e.g., becoming more aware of blind spots)
- encouraging experimentation with new techniques that you might not have considered or attempted on your own

- providing encouragement: boredom and frustration are part of the learning process, but if we give up at any sign of these, we're doing ourselves a disservice—a coach can be your cheerleader and task master rolled into one.

Investing in this kind of self-improvement is a win-win. Not only is it deeply satisfying to feel that you are growing and bettering yourself, but you are accomplishing more, contributing more, and ultimately benefiting others.

Go for Flow

Kaya Dorey was a quiet "back row" kid in one of the Climate Change courses I taught, never getting too involved in any of the classroom discussions. So, imagine my surprise when, for one assignment, she submitted a stop-motion animated film featuring original artwork, voice-over narration, and a hilarious storyline involving a sleuth of snowmobile-riding polar bears. Actually, I wasn't surprised—I was blown away. The amount of focus and time that went into this assignment was well above what was asked for. What was it about this project that had made the difference for Kaya?

It would be years later when I got my answer. The next time I spoke with Kaya, she was running her own business, Novel Supply Co., which makes stylish, sustainable clothing using ethically sourced materials and processes that are safe for the environment.

The amount of work it took to get her own business up and running was immense, and although there are tedious aspects to running a business, Kaya finds rewards each step of the way. "When I am immersed in work that I love, it's like time doesn't exist," she told me. "It happened to me the other day when I was doing some natural dyeing at my studio." Kaya described the very scientific process of mixing the components and the different processes the fabric must undergo to me. It sounded very complicated, but Kaya's voice was all passion and enthusiasm. "I was mesmerized by the fabric turning from green to blue within seconds. I forgot about all the unanswered emails, the blog post due the next day, and the accounting that had to be done. All I saw was indigo. I dipped each batch of garments twice, and by the time I was done, the sun was setting [and I] realized how late it was."

As she spoke, I knew I was witnessing the same energy and passion that she had poured into her class project. Kaya was a woman who knew how to drop into flow. And if you've ever experienced moments like this, where you seem to lose track of the world and time while immersed in the task at hand, then you know just how sweet it is.

Hungarian American psychologist Mihaly Csikszentmihalyi performed pioneering research in the area of mental states. "Flow" is how he described the experience of being so involved in an activity that time seems to disappear. It's the feeling that can occur while undertaking a challenging activity that matches your skill level—not too easy, and not so difficult that you can't complete it. Often, people in the midst of a flow experience get so caught up in the activity that their sense of self seems to evaporate, and the feeling of time gets distorted; minutes can feel like hours, and hours can feel like minutes. The sense of entering a flow state has been reported across pursuits as diverse as dancing, surgery, rock climbing, and chess playing. Flow is achieved when passion and skills meet to take on a challenge, and it can feel like a moment of magic. But that doesn't mean it can't be intentionally generated, too.

Flow happens for me when I'm immersed in creative work, like lesson planning, brainstorming a community project, or writing an article. Because I'm typically at my best in the mornings, I begin setting the stage for flow's arrival the night before by getting to bed at a decent hour. I awake feeling fresh and energized, and after a little exercise, coffee, and a light breakfast, I reduce any noise in the room and put my phone on quiet mode. I save emails, administration, and other less intensive tasks for the afternoons (when I'm not as alert), then I sit down and put pen to paper. Flow doesn't happen instantly, but I have done all I can to produce an optimal environment—and if I am fully attentive to my work, more often than not, I will enter flow. It's so enjoyable, and my productivity is much higher than at other times. The rewarding feelings that arise from flow also motivate me to forge ahead with the more challenging, or less satisfying, elements of my work.

Flow is not to be expected 100 percent of the time—but identifying and cultivating an environment that produces more flow states in your life will increase your enjoyment and satisfaction, which ultimately fosters a greater sense of purpose.

Remember that stocking your toolkit is a lifelong process. And although we can feel prepared for a journey, quest, or project, we won't really know until we're in action, witnessing it ourselves. Then we can see our progress and understand what steps we have to take next.

To return to my previous analogy, every good musician needs passion, skills, a trusted teacher, and many thousands of hours of practice over their career. But, although you can experience a lot of enjoyment and satisfaction making music on your own, it is ultimately the experience of playing in front of an audience that will unleash your true potential and contribute something of value to the world. So, get out there and *just do it!*

Week 3 Lesson Summary

- When you apply your abilities to things you care about, you can make a real impact. But first, take stock of what's in your toolkit. Notice what may be missing, and then get to work on filling the gaps.
- Try adopting a beginner's mindset. Nothing stimulates learning quite like a willingness to try and fail. Dive in and get messy!
- Good things take time, so keep up that growth mindset. It's the plain truth to say, "I'm just learning how to do this, so of course I'm not good at it…yet! With practice, I am bound to improve."

- An experienced coach or training program can help you achieve your best through proven strategies and techniques.
- Go for flow! The flow state provides the payoff for developing and applying your skills to meaningful projects. Not only do your efforts help to create something of value, but you get to experience these deeply satisfying immersive states when doing so.

Week 3 Exercises

1. WHAT'S IN YOUR TOOLKIT?

Grab your pen and paper and get ready to start listing the skills you currently have. Think about your talents, training, knowledge, and experience. Consider the following questions: What are your existing competencies? What skills do you get complimented on the most? What comes naturally or easily to you that is challenging for others? What do people come to you for? You can also return to your list of passions from last week. There is a good chance you have already started developing skills related to the things you love. Pay special attention to those in particular. Tip: Consider both hard and soft skills. Hard skills are abilities that are easy to quantify, like speaking a foreign language, operating a machine, using computer software, or playing an instrument. Soft skills are more subjective. They are sometimes called "people skills" or "interpersonal skills" because they have to do with human relationships. Some examples include teamwork, communication, flexibility, patience, and time management.

2. WHAT TOOLS ARE YOU MISSING?

The odds are good that as you listed the skills you have, you also started to take note of some skills that you'd like to have. Make a list of whatever comes to mind. Now, pick the top three skills that you're interested in learning.

If you wrote down "learn Italian," consider how you'll use it and what level you'd like to attain. Are you looking to be able to order a meal during your next vacation, or are you going for fluency because it's your dream to work in Italy? How long are you willing to work on this skill? Three months? A year? More?

Once you have an idea of what you'd like to achieve, the final step is to ask yourself if they can be broken down into smaller chunks (sub-skills). Think about how you'll gain these skills: from a course, a trainer, by volunteering, watching instructional videos, reading, or a combination?

3. CONSIDER A COACH

The right coaching relationship can fast-track your development. Do you have a respected peer or colleague who might be available to you in this capacity? Think of someone whom you admire and trust, and who would be a good fit for you. Have a conversation and see if it makes sense to ask this person to coach you. Remember to make your ask as specific and clear as possible. What skills do you want to work on? What results are you hoping to achieve? How long do you expect the process to take?

4. CULTIVATE FLOW

Don't wait for flow to happen by chance, but take deliberate steps to cultivate these states throughout the week. Reflect on past moments of flow where you lost track of time and became immersed in the task at hand. What were you doing? Was it morning, afternoon, or evening? Experiment with optimizing your environment to allow for more of these flow states. Do you like to work when it's quiet? With music? In a busy café? Are you better after a workout? Do you have any favorite scents? Play with your senses.

Weekly Challenge: Sharpen Your Skills

To start developing a growth mindset, this week's challenge is to practice a new skill for at least thirty minutes each day. Go back to your list of three skills that you would like to learn from Exercise 2. Select one that you want to work on this week. If you have not already broken it down into sub-skills, then do so now, and select one of those tasks that you could practice daily.

For instance, if you want to play the piano, "doing scales" could be a sub-skill for daily practice. Or if you want to improve your communication skills, you could schedule one short conversation a day with a friend to work on eye contact and reflect back what the person shares with you.

For the sake of this exercise, the skill itself is secondary, so don't overthink it. The important thing is that you get yourself into the habit. Repeat, repeat, repeat! Now, get out your calendar and schedule in those practice sessions.

Note: Practicing can often be fun, but it can just as often be dull, so you may be tempted to give up. But the magic happens when you hang in there. You are developing a growth mindset, so just remind yourself it's okay to screw up when you're a beginner, and remember that if you believe your abilities grow as you use them, then you will certainly improve.

Don't forget to journal about your experiences with this weekly challenge before moving on to Week 4. For more direction, refer to the guide for self-reflection in the Appendix.

WEEK 4

SERVICE: LEAVING FOOTPRINTS

**The best way to find yourself is to lose
yourself in the service of others.**
– MAHATMA GANDHI

Footprints. Somebody's been here.
– INDIANA JONES*

MARKUS PUKONEN IS SOMEONE WHO LIKES TO DIVE INTO LIFE.
This is literally what he did when he leapt from the side of a sailboat
a thousand miles off the coast of North America. Alone, treading water in
the middle of the Pacific Ocean, his unaccompanied vessel swayed in the
waves several yards behind him. He snapped a selfie as he floated before
casually swimming back to his boat.

The blond, goateed seafarer struck me as a modern-day mash-up of
Marco Polo and Huckleberry Finn as he regaled me with tales of his solo

---

**Indiana Jones and the Kingdom of the Crystal Skull* (2008) travels on the *Dolce*, a 1968 Alberg thirty-foot sailboat, from Vancouver Island to Hawaii. This alone impressed me, but it was only a small part of a 49,700-mile, self-powered, multiyear expedition that he named Routes of Change. Raising awareness and money for nonprofits and charities focused on justice and sustainability in the regions he visits, he is doing his entire trip without getting on an airplane, in a car, or using any other motorized mode of transportation. He's sailed. He's paddled. He's pedaled. He's walked. He's crawled. He even bounced on a pogo stick (for a whopping 6.2 miles across Winnipeg, Manitoba). Using all these forms of nonmotorized transportation is fun, helps to relieve the monotony of travel, and puts a creative spin on his effort to embrace more sustainable ways of living.

When I spoke with Markus, he was in Honolulu, equipping the *Dolce* for the next leg of his journey—a three-week, 2,200-mile voyage to the Marshall Islands. I asked what had compelled him to embark on his odyssey.

"I spent most of my twenties doing seasonal work and traveling overseas in my spare time," he said. "It was fun, but something didn't feel right. I wasn't living up to my potential. I felt the need to be more creative, more active, and to give more of my energy to the world.

"Then my dad was diagnosed with leukemia and given weeks to live."

When I heard this, the feeling that arose in me was all too familiar. I could intensely relate to what he told me next. He was in shock, which led him to do some deep self-questioning. What if his own death was imminent? How would he want to spend his last days?

Routes of Change was Markus's answer. Through this work, he found a way to harness his love of travel, adventure, and filmmaking to generate exposure for people working to create a healthier, kinder planet. As he moves from place to place, Markus connects with leaders of grassroots social and environmental organizations, helping to raise money for them through donations collected on his website and sharing their stories through presentations, videos, social media, and other channels. "There are amazing people all over the planet who are working for the common good, but often they're unsung heroes," he explained. "I'm in a unique position to find these people and raise support for them due to the slow way in which I travel. It's a combination of everything I'm passionate about, expressed as honestly as I know how."

For the previous three weeks, our path to personal growth has focused largely inward. This week, we will examine the concept of service. This powerful agent of change has the potential to cause ripples, both outward and inward, with feelings of connection, peace, and fulfillment.

We all leave footprints in the sands of time. The impact we have on others and the world around us is our legacy. For better or for worse, each of us affects our community and the planet we live on, even through the actions of our everyday lives. If we want our impact to be a positive one, we need to remember that what we do matters—but *how* we do it, the joy we bring to it, and how it aligns with our best selves, also matters.

Now, perhaps Markus's example is so dramatic that it feels out of reach to you. Not everyone has the inclination or means to do something on that scale. You don't need to make massive changes in your life to begin practicing acts of service. It can be as simple as noticing what you need in your own life and starting there.

Give What You Need

Leigh Schumann is a fundraising and communications consultant to nonprofit organizations, and the former executive director of a Vancouver-based grassroots charity called The Lipstick Project, which she founded after spending a year in Ethiopia. On contract with a nongovernmental organization (NGO) as a communications officer, she felt she was doing important work, but she also found that she was lonely. Looking for a way to fill the void, Leigh decided to volunteer in her spare time. She reached out to a hospital in the area that treated women injured during childbirth.

The doctors didn't need any extra help with routine medical care, but they suggested that she could assist by spending time with the women on Sunday afternoons. After brainstorming over the phone with friends back home, she came up with an idea. Why not do manicures, just like she and her pals would do on weekends?

"So, there I was the next Sunday with a few bottles of nail polish, some hand lotion, and a nail file," Leigh said. "To say that it wasn't awkward would be a lie, but as we got used to each other and the weeks passed, our Sunday Spas became an event we all looked forward to."

Through this simple act of service, Leigh witnessed the solace that came with gentle touch. "Human touch helps people to know they're not alone, that someone is there with them, focused on them, and reminding them that they matter." These sessions created genuine, heartfelt connections that decreased the women's sense of isolation and loneliness—and cured Leigh's loneliness, too.

Leigh was so deeply impacted by this experience that, upon her arrival home, she was determined to bring these benefits to her own community as well. She started The Lipstick Project in 2012 to provide free, professional spa services—manicures, pedicures, hair services, and massages—to the terminally ill. The charity's mission was to bring comfort and dignity to people in the last days of their lives, through something as simple as loving attention and touch. The Lipstick Project closed in 2019, but its legacy continues to this day; the hospitals and hospices it served now coordinate volunteer salon and spa professionals directly.

Leigh found success by tapping into the simple truth that small acts can make an enormous difference in the lives of others. And when we give to the world what we need, it will return to us tenfold. This is a very empowering practice.

Start Where You Are

You may be daunted by the thought of devoting a lot of time to a service project. So, what about considering your job itself? The average person spends approximately ninety thousand hours at work over their lifetime. Assuming eight hours of sleep a night, this equates to one-third of your total waking hours over a fifty-year working life. That's a lot of time that could be put toward satisfying and meaningful contributions.

At the age of eighteen, Angela Nagy had an epiphany while on a camping trip with her father. She had recently secured her first job with the municipal government in Kelowna, British Columbia, as a grants coordinator. The position was quite a responsibility for a teenager, but she wasn't sure if it fit in with her life ambitions, which, as she was barely out of high school, were still forming. Her first project was to help preserve a park along an ecologically sensitive riverbank, which exposed her to the shocking reality of human-caused damage to the ecosystem. The project was successful, but it opened Angela's eyes to the alarming fact that there were no strict environmental policies in place. What would the riverbank look like in another fifty years without any protective measures? This question hovered in her mind that night as she lay in the grass in the campground, after her father had gone to sleep.

She gazed up at the countless stars and thought about her own path in life. There were so many options; which one to choose? As a young woman, Angela's whole working life lay ahead of her. How was she to decide which path would be the right one—not only to fulfill her potential, but to help ensure the health of the natural world around her? With the ground beneath her and the sky above, it was clear. Angela decided right then to commit her career, in whatever form it would take, to protecting the environment.

Fast-forward to today, and Angela has made good on her teenage promise. After working for the City of Kelowna, Angela got a job with an environmentally focused marketing firm, where she worked in advertising, marketing, and account management. Later, she joined a tech start-up that did wastewater monitoring. Eventually, she became the top-performing salesperson at the company. "I treated these jobs like my own business," Angela explained, when I asked how she worked her way up. "I took on responsibilities beyond my job description and owned my work and my clients' satisfaction. Working for two start-ups taught me to wear many hats, and I learned from my employers' successes and mistakes."

In 2008, at the age of thirty, she was elected a city councillor (after running for office six times) and cofounded GreenStep Solutions, a consulting company that helps small- and medium-sized businesses increase profits while improving their sustainability performance. She left municipal politics at thirty-three and has since focused on building GreenStep. Her professional achievements, along with an impressive track record in community volunteerism, earned Angela the Mayor's Environmental Achievement Award for the most environmentally dedicated individual in Kelowna. Judging by her many accomplishments, she's most certainly made that eighteen-year-old proud.

Angela's not alone in being motivated by a desire to effect positive change. Increasingly, today's workers are driven by a search for meaning, connection, and the opportunity to leave a legacy. A survey of more than 7,800 millennials from twenty-nine countries found that 60 percent of respondents identified a "sense of purpose" as part of the reason they chose their current job.

When you feel that your work contributes to something bigger, you wake up energized and excited about the day ahead. You're more engaged, motivated, satisfied, and fulfilled, both on and off the job. This is not only good news for you, but for your employer as well.

Like individuals, organizations can prosper when their strategies and direction are informed by core values that extend beyond generating profits. They're then able to attract and retain the best talent; and with this congruency of values, everyone is happier and more productive, which drives up profits and allows for raises, promotions, bonuses, and other perks that ultimately build an upward spiral of success.

We tend to think of the helping professions (medicine, social services, teaching, firefighting, etc.) and charities as making differences in the world. But many careers allow you to contribute to the greater good. Angela Nagy isn't physically out in the rivers making the water clean; she works in an office, making decisions that set off whole chains of events. Policymakers, technologists, farmers, clinical researchers, journalists, and architects don't typically interact with the consumers of their services, but their work still impacts their lives—and our broader society. Consider the scientists at Upside Foods (previously Memphis Meats), the Californian biotechnology company that makes cruelty-free meat directly from cultured animal cells. As an alternative to conventionally produced meat, their method of growing meat in a laboratory eliminates the need to raise and process animals or use huge amounts of land and water. By providing consumers with a humanely and sustainably created product that tastes good and is progressively becoming cost competitive, they are working toward their ultimate vision of "a world where every person can eat delicious food, without compromise," according to the company's website. That's certainly a good reason to get up in the morning!

Now, perhaps you didn't have an epiphany on your path, or a passion at an early age, and are already in a job that leaves you feeling disconnected from any larger purpose. You may simply have to look at it from another angle. Ditchdiggers, sanitation workers, housekeepers, and salesclerks are often overlooked workers who provide critical services for the greater good of everyone. Every job provides possibilities for meaningful contribution, but what if you feel it's still not enough?

Why not look into volunteering or service opportunities that may be available through your employer? Many companies have social responsibility programs like food drives, days off for volunteering, or team-building exercises that also raise money for charity. Find out what exists at your workplace and get involved in something that appeals to you, or spearhead a new initiative.

Granted, it's not always easy to trigger changes within an organization; and it takes time to transition to a new position, company, or career path. The reality is that there may be times in your life when work doesn't seem particularly meaningful or fulfilling. That's fine. Remember that old "Ride mule, chase horse" saying? Working for a paycheck is respectable; just don't let too many days (or years) pass by without doing anything about it, or you may end up apathetic and resistant to change. Take a course, upgrade your credentials, network with professionals in other companies or fields, get a coach or mentor, and devise a plan to escape career purgatory.

Consider Angela's advice: "If you love your job, stay there and find ways to make a difference within the organization. If you don't love your work, maybe it's time to pivot or take a leap toward the job of your dreams. There are many purpose-driven organizations that need passionate people, and the more you can do while also ensuring that your own needs are met, the better our world will become."

But remember, work is only one of many avenues to contribute to a better world.

The Rewards of Volunteering

Volunteering is one of the most common avenues of service, and it's not just a great thing to do—it's good for you, too! Humans seem hardwired to gain pleasure from altruism and philanthropy. So, volunteering can create positive feelings for us in and of itself, as well as benefiting others. Multiple studies have found that volunteering is linked to improved life satisfaction and well-being, and lower levels of depression. The happiness boost you get from volunteering also creates a positive feedback loop. Happier people are more likely to give their time and lend a hand to others, even complete strangers. So, the more you give, the more you want to keep giving.

But who has the time?

For many people with busy lives, giving time is a challenge. It feels like a cost we're not always willing to pay. But how about viewing it differently? I believe it's better to think of volunteering as an investment, rather than a cost. Investing your time in a cause, or in others, pays off in countless ways throughout the community. What's more, it can also lead to a healthier, happier, and more fulfilling life for you. In my book, that's time well spent.

I'd argue that most among the professional-managerial class could spare at least a couple of extra hours in the week to volunteer. This doesn't necessarily mean in a formal capacity with an organization, as there are many ways to volunteer informally; it simply means unpaid time that you give to anyone, outside of your family, who's in need. Personally, I could easily give up some of the time I spend in front of the television or surfing the web. Shifting this "wasted" time to more meaningful activities isn't hard. It just takes some discipline and dedication. Remember that when your values and passions are aligned, you'll experience both the motivation and the reward.

There are other perks to volunteering, aside from simply the good feelings it will generate. You can pick up new skills, for instance. And for emerging professionals or those considering a new career path, it's a good way to explore different fields and improve career options while demonstrating your work ethic and values to potential employers.

If you're already firmly established in your work, it's also a great way to expand your social circle and meet people from different backgrounds. I had a profound firsthand experience of this a few years ago when I volunteered with the Union Gospel Mission, an urban relief organization based in Vancouver's Downtown Eastside.

The Downtown Eastside is one of Canada's most impoverished neighborhoods and is known for its high rates of homelessness, drug addiction, survival sex work, crime, and violence. Previously, I hadn't spent much time in the area, and my perception of it was not good.

I won't sugarcoat it. My time volunteering at the mission was intense, especially when participating in their Street Light and Mobile Mission programs, which took us out into the neighborhood to provide food, water, and other basics to people living on the streets. It was tough to see the sometimes violent behavior, psychological turmoil, hunger, and other struggles of people on the street. And it was eye-opening to witness how the homeless are both seen and not seen by other citizens.

In Vancouver, if you stay off certain streets in the city, then the homeless are largely invisible. But if you do look, what you see isn't pretty. We allow their humanity to be eclipsed by problems like poverty, addiction, and mental illness. We forget to extend the same respect we give our neighbors, forgetting that these people are our neighbors, too.

Even though I think of myself as an open-minded and accepting person, thoughts did flash across my mind about how people end up on the street. I questioned how much responsibility we have for our own situation, individually and collectively. And I concluded that there are no easy answers. Circumstances and events are often beyond our control, and there are gaps in our social safety net and healthcare system that, unfortunately, allow bad things to happen to good people.

At the drop-in center one morning, I talked with a man who had stopped in for some assistance. Clean-shaven and bright-eyed, he didn't look like someone I'd imagine having trouble making ends meet. But he candidly discussed the challenges of living on social assistance in Vancouver, one of the most expensive cities in North America. After accounting for shelter, his government income assistance provided him with less than ten dollars a day for food, transportation, and other expenses. It was 8 a.m. and I had already spent almost that amount on transit and coffee.

Volunteering at UGM was deeply rewarding and enlightening. It pushed me out of my comfort zone and made me reflect on my earlier misconceptions of the neighborhood as a place to be avoided. Connecting with some of its residents helped me to see a subtler side of the community. There is a wonderful sense of belonging, resilience, and resourcefulness that shows in the way people care for one another. This could stand as a model for how we might all build better communities and a better world.

Leverage Your Skills

Just as every job has the potential for service and growth, so too does every volunteering opportunity. But that doesn't mean you shouldn't be selective. I already mentioned that when your values and passions are aligned while volunteering, you'll experience both motivation and reward. When you bring your own set of unique skills to the experience as well, get ready for real change.

In 2010, Mark Horoszowski left his job at a marketing agency in Seattle to travel around the world for a year and volunteer. His plan was to offer his marketing and business skills to local NGOs in the countries that he visited. At first, he questioned if he'd be able to find suitable opportunities that fit his travel itinerary, but he soon realized his worries were unfounded. He discovered many nonprofits seeking help with specific creative, technical, and business tasks, and struggling to find volunteers with the necessary proficiency. The problem: individuals with the required capabilities aren't always in proximity, and even if these people are searching for volunteer opportunities, there's no guarantee they will stumble upon the organization in need.

This planted the seed for a business idea. Through a chance meeting, Mark connected with fellow globetrotter Derk Norde. Together, they spent the next year creating a global platform called MovingWorlds, which connects skilled professionals with volunteering opportunities all over the globe (they refer to their volunteers as "experteers"). Think of it like a short-term Peace Corps for people with specialized professional experience. Since its launch in 2011, MovingWorlds has helped deliver millions of dollars' worth of professional skills to social enterprises and NGOs in more than thirty countries.

MovingWorlds employs a win-win strategy that recognizes both the needs of volunteers to contribute valuable skills and the rights of a community to receive what's needed. The complicated world of charitable giving is often driven by donors' wishes, and recipient organizations can end up with gifts they cannot use, e.g., a goat, when they need an accountant for their office. It can be politically fraught. But MovingWorlds is brilliantly different.

When I asked Mark to share a success story, he told me about Deana, a user-experience designer who worked at a major corporation in the United States. She had a one-week vacation on the horizon and wanted to spend it helping others while immersing herself in a foreign culture. Volunteering was the ticket to getting the most out of her short break. She applied to MovingWorlds and was placed with Maya Traditions, a social enterprise in Guatemala that connects female Indigenous artisans with national and international markets. Their work helps to create economic and educational opportunities for the women and their families through preserving and promoting traditional Mayan art and culture. Once on the ground in Guatemala, Deana helped to plan a new website to increase exposure of their local, artisanal products. She stayed engaged virtually after returning home and ended up mentoring two other experteers involved in the project.

Talking to Mark made me reflect on my own experiences. Much of my past volunteer work has involved physical activity, ranging from picking up donated food and other products from stores to organizing and moving inventory, and working in kitchens to prep and serve meals. In my day job, much of my time is spent on a computer, so I welcomed the physical nature of this work. Rather than feeling drained and foggy headed after hours on a computer, I finished my volunteer shifts feeling energized. Still, apart from the health benefits, was this the most effective use of my time? Could I have made a greater impact doing something else?

When contemplating these questions, it's worth considering the value of your time. If you follow the stock market, you'll know that different financial investments produce different yields. This is also true of your time. The following example comes from my own experience. Option A: Serve coffee and snacks at a homeless shelter. Option B: Lead an interactive workshop for adults with cognitive disabilities.

I have done both activities, and each cause is important, but the first didn't require a distinct skill set, whereas the second one did—and I matched it. It can be argued that the second option provided better value to the recipients because of my skills. And although I say to leverage your most valuable talents for maximum impact, this is not a hard-and-fast rule. I enjoyed both volunteering options; remember, when doing things the Gandhiana Jones way, enjoyment counts. If you'd feel happier serving coffee, then by all means, serve coffee.

Perhaps it is time to realize that concepts like "selfish" and "selfless" are outdated. Pursuing your own happiness is not a selfish action, nor should helping others be something you do to benefit them without considering your own well-being. Positive emotions are what fuel you to keep contributing. And remember Leigh Schumann's lesson—never underestimate the power of the small. You never know the chain of events that could follow that cup of coffee you serve. Maybe it could end up changing someone's life in a way you can't yet see.

The Boomerang Effect

Speaking of the power of the small, I've offered a lot of examples of big contributions, but the simple practice of spreading kindness can have a huge impact as well.

The drive-through lane of a fast-food joint might not be the first thing that comes to mind when considering how to better the world. In many ways, drive-throughs epitomize our hurried, disconnected North American culture. That said, one December morning in 2012, a customer in Winnipeg decided to pay for the order of the next vehicle in a drive-through line up; the patron who benefited from that act of generosity decided to pick up the tab for the next car. One after another, customers followed suit in a cascade of kindness that lasted for three hours, including 228 orders in all.

When we benefit from kindness, we are moved to "pay it forward." The origin of this term is unclear, but it describes what could almost be defined as a law of human behavior. Kindness leads to happiness, which leads to more kindness, in a virtuous circle. Studies show that even when we merely witness an act of kindness, we feel our emotions lift and are motivated to be altruistic. The effect can spread through a community, increasing the sense of connection and well-being of its members.

Being kind to people we know well is an easy sell. Most of us like helping our friends, and it strengthens our existing bonds. But it's not always instinctive to be altruistic toward strangers, especially when you're busily occupied with your own concerns. However, kindness toward anyone at all will make you happy by increasing levels of the neurotransmitter dopamine in the brain. This feeling of exhilaration, known as "helper's high," increases your energy and boosts your sense of well-being. Studies also show that regular acts of kindness can help reduce blood pressure, lower the risk of heart disease, reduce excess stomach acid, and relieve pain, among other health benefits.

In short, kindness has a boomerang effect; the more you give, the more comes back to you, down to the smallest act. Want to test this out for yourself? Consider the act of smiling. Next time you're walking along a busy sidewalk, smile warmly to a passing stranger. Odds are, you'll receive a smile in return, which triggers a flood of positive sensations within. And, as it turns out, that smile may be more powerful than you know. Ron Gutman, an entrepreneur and thought leader in health and innovation, delivered a fascinating TED Talk on the hidden powers of smiling. According to Gutman, smiling on a regular basis can lower stress, reduce blood pressure, and enhance your mood. One smile can generate the equivalent brain stimulation to eating two thousand bars of chocolate— but without the cost or the calories. There's even evidence that smiling is linked with longer life expectancy. Smiling, like kindness, makes you feel good, and is contagious in the best way.

Release Expectations

Not all acts of kindness generate such obviously positive results as the Winnipeg drive-through or the exchange of smiles between two passersby. Sometimes, they can look like they've failed utterly. One Sunday morning a few years ago, I decided to surprise my fellow apartment dwellers with a small treat. In our building's lobby, I left a gift certificate good for multiple coffees at the neighborhood café. On a sign next to it, I'd written in bold lettering:

"Hi, neighbors! Treat yourself to a coffee at the café across the street, then please return the gift card for someone else to use. Enjoy!"

The gift card was taken within half an hour, but it was not returned. I left the sign up for a few days to appeal to the culprit's better nature, but it was never to be seen again.

This act of kindness yielded disappointing results. At first, I was upset, but I soon realized I'd been attached to the results, relying on a positive outcome. This is a setup for disappointment. Praise, or other rewards of some kind, would have validated my actions and made me feel great, but my higher self knew that I couldn't expect others to play nice. I could do my thing, hoping for a positive outcome, but I would then need to let go of what happened next. I would do it for the sake of doing it. Nothing more.

Realigned with my values, I looked for a different opportunity to spread some kindness in my building. Figuring that most property managers only hear complaints or requests from their tenants, I dropped off a thank-you card for the woman in charge of my apartment building. It noted her diligent efforts, responsiveness, and attention to detail in dealing with all the past issues at my apartment. A couple of days later, I was pleasantly surprised to receive a warm note of acknowledgment. Her simple, unexpected gesture made my day, as mine had hers.

Just as a single seed can bloom into a flower, a simple act of kindness can become something beautiful, if you share freely. You don't have to save the world, figure it all out, or commit a lot of time out of your busy life. Just come from your heart. What has made a difference to you today? Thank your bus driver, chat with the person next to you at the supermarket checkout, or leave encouraging comments on social media to express your gratitude and appreciation of others. These simple acts can open everyone's heart—even just a little bit—and they feel so good. After a while, you'll realize how natural and easy this practice is, and you just won't want to stop.

Look to the Trees

Not long ago, I heard something interesting about trees. In a forest, trees share nutrients and water through an underground network, with the bigger trees feeding the younger ones, making the entire community of trees stronger.

Inspired by this thought one day, I spent an hour in contemplation in the forest behind the university where I teach. It was a gray and drizzly day. But, instead of feeling bleak and alone, I saw the world around me in a different way.

Inhaling the oxygen-rich air and regarding the beauty of the forest around me, I saw the web of life that each of us is a part of. We are indeed all connected. The art of being human and living a life of purpose (dare I say, a spiritual life) is to nurture those connections in service of something greater than ourselves. Personal growth and fulfillment don't happen in a bubble. Like a living, breathing forest, we need each other in order to thrive. By working collectively, we make each other stronger and create something vaster than any of us could build alone.

If you are looking for more meaning in your life, branch out and connect to others to find how you can bring your values, passions, and skills together to serve others in ways that create positive effects for everyone involved. The impact you can have is something beyond measure, but without a doubt, your footprints will leave a lasting impression.

Week 4 Lesson Summary

- We all leave a legacy, like footprints in the sand. Be aware of where you're leaving footprints and strive to make them positive ones.
- The hidden payoff of contributing to the outer world is receiving tangible benefits to your inner life. And often, when we give what we need, we get what we need in return.
- Cultivate a sense of purpose in your profession. Feeling like your work serves a higher goal (beyond making money) helps with motivation and engagement. This can lead to a happier, more fulfilled, and ultimately more productive life, on and off the job.
- Volunteer. Being of service to others is a solid investment in your own growth, too.
- Leverage your skill set to create a positive impact. For maximum effect, look for opportunities to make use of your most valuable skills.

- Make kindness a regular part of your day. Small, simple acts can bring joy to others and make a difference in ways you can't imagine.
- Watch your expectations. Not every attempt to make a difference will be successful. Base your satisfaction on knowing you're driven by your higher principles.

Week 4 Exercises

1. GIVE WHAT YOU NEED

List three things that would be helpful to you, or that you would like more of in your life. These can range from small needs (someone to play your favorite board game with) to large (more accessible green spaces in your community). Pick one item and brainstorm some ways to give this very thing to others.

2. FIND PURPOSE IN YOUR WORK

Answer the following questions:

- Does your job contribute to a greater purpose? If so, can you name it?
- How might you be of service to your coworkers outside of your position's responsibilities?
- Does your employer offer opportunities to volunteer outside of the company, or to make a difference in other ways? How can you get involved?

If you're currently in school or looking for a job, or if you're considering a career change, then answer the following questions:

- What values do you want your next employer to have?
- If you have a specific employer in mind, do you know their mission statement or greater purpose? Does it align with your passion and sense of purpose?

3. LET'S VOLUNTEER

It's now time to consider some possible volunteering opportunities that align with your values, passions, and skills. Do some brainstorming. What do you love to do? What do you do well? And what do you care about in the world? Write about the passions, skills, and causes that are important to you, and you may see connections emerge. There are no bad ideas, so let them fly!

4. WHAT DO OTHERS NEED?

Try an experiment. Post on social media that you are looking to donate some time to anyone who needs help with something. It can be a fun way to reconnect with a friend you haven't seen in a while, or to get to know someone better while helping them out at the same time.

5. SPREAD KINDNESS

Brainstorm some random acts of kindness you could perform this week. Start by writing about what you like doing and how you already spend your time: work, commuting, meals, pets, exercise, phone calls, socializing, home repairs, etc. Consider how you can connect with friends and family in one or more of these areas, in some small, helpful way. Have some fun with this. Imagine doing something totally unexpected that would surprise someone in the best way possible!

Weekly Challenge: Be of Service

Your challenge this week is to spend at least thirty minutes each day doing things that contribute to the world around you.

Look at the results of your brainstorming session and pick something new to do each day. It could be a few small things that add up to thirty minutes, or one thing that takes that long. Have fun—it's not just a fringe benefit, it's part of this challenge!

There are many ways to contribute, and you don't need to commit a huge amount of time in order to make a difference for others. Although some of us might want to undertake a substantial project, for many of us, contributing just means taking consistent actions in our personal and professional lives. Start small by opening the door for someone, carrying a fellow customer's groceries to the car, or buying a stranger a cup of coffee. Or jump right in and fix a friend's flat tire. Use your best skills by helping friends declutter their homes or do their taxes. On an even larger scale, you could help serve meals at a homeless shelter, or spearhead a neighborhood park cleanup day. No action is too large or too small.

The karmic payoff for all your work this week? Not only will your efforts help make the world a better place for everyone, they will lead to a better life for you, too—one that is happier, healthier, and more fulfilled. It's the ultimate win-win.

Tip: Make a log of your daily contributions. Happiness increases simply by counting your own acts of service or kindness. I recommend doing this in the evening to give yourself a boost at the end of the day.

Don't forget to journal about your experiences with this weekly challenge before moving on to Week 5. For more direction, refer to the guide for self-reflection in the Appendix.

THE FOUR PRINCIPLES IN HARMONY

CERTAIN HISTORIC EVENTS HAVE SUCH GRAVITY THAT THE exact moment you heard about them becomes forever crystallized in your memory. Some notable examples: the assassination of President Kennedy; the first manned mission to land on the moon; the Space Shuttle Challenger disaster; the death of Princess Diana; and the presidential inauguration of Barack Obama. Depending on your age, you may be able to recall with astonishing clarity where you were and what you were doing when you first heard about events such as these.

Unquestionably, one of the biggest "Where were you when...?" moments in recent history is when al-Qaeda terrorists attacked the World Trade Center on Tuesday, September 11, 2001—a day that has been immortalized as 9/11. My own memory of that fateful day will be forever linked to a certain photograph, now considered to be one of the most iconic images of 9/11.

The Falling Man, a photograph by Richard Drew, shows an unidentified man plummeting from the upper levels of the North Tower of the World Trade Center. The photo gives the impression that the man is in a rigid headfirst dive, with one leg slightly bent and his body in near-perfect symmetry with the stark skyscraper behind him (though the full series of photos reveals that he is actually tumbling through the air). The photograph is terrifying, disturbing, and difficult to look at. However, it is also somehow cathartic for me. As time goes by, it gets easier to disconnect from the horrors and heartbreak of that day. But this photo, with its harsh imagery, does not let me forget. It serves as a reminder, on a purely visceral level, of what took place.

I was fascinated by the capacity of photographs like *The Falling Man* to visually communicate the raw human emotions associated with 9/11. A short time later, these thoughts provided the spark for an idea. What if photographs, as well as being powerfully haunting, could also be *healing?* With the right intention, could photography serve as a force for betterment?

It struck me that photography could be used on a large scale to effect change in my community. If enough people joined in and took photographs that expressed positive sentiments, and shared these photos widely, then together, we could make a difference in the well-being of the community. Or so my thinking went.

The idea took root, and I sketched out the plans for a citywide project called Expressions of Humanity. Its aim was to encourage people to convey acts of compassion, love, and kindness through photographs, which would then be exhibited in local publications and public spaces. This was before social media, so the scope was naturally constrained.

Expressions of Humanity was a passion project for me, and because I had to squeeze it in outside of working hours, there was no way I could do it alone. I also wanted to raise money and bring awareness to a good cause, so I sought to partner with an established charity.

Over lunch one day, a friend suggested that I consider Habitat for Humanity, the nonprofit group that builds affordable housing for families in need. At the time, I was only aware of the organization's international work to build homes in African and Asian countries. I was surprised to learn that Habitat had more than three thousand affiliate branches all over the world, including one located in Vancouver. I phoned up the local affiliate, and a few days later, I was in their office to share my idea. They liked my vision for the project and agreed to partner with me to make it a reality.

Together, we launched the first annual Expressions of Humanity event. Numerous companies came on board to sponsor the project and donate amazing prizes for the top photos. Media outlets sponsored the project, too, giving us free ad space for promotion and spots to display the photographs. The project wrapped up with a major gala, and the photos were exhibited in public spaces around the city. We ran the event annually for four years.

I loved being involved in the project and hearing the heart-touching stories that emerged. One year, a photo titled *Binners' Dinners* was submitted by photographer Jaleen Grove. The image shows a homeless man, whose name is Tex, standing in a back alley amid several dumpsters. Next to him is a shopping cart full of items he's salvaged from the garbage. The photograph depicted the resourcefulness and enterprising spirit of street-involved people. Tex had granted his permission for Grove to submit the portrait to the contest, on the condition that if it won, the prize, whatever it was, would be donated back to Habitat for Humanity. And win it did—*Binners' Dinners* took first place that year. The prize was a trip for two to Mexico, but Tex was true to his word, so it was donated back to the charity and auctioned off to raise even more funds.

When asked why he donated his prize, Tex said, "They need it more than I do," referring to the families who are supported by Habitat's work. "It's funny, here I am living on the street and look what happened. I won a trip to Mexico and gave it back."

His generosity was humbling, especially considering his personal circumstances. Tex lived on the streets in Vancouver's inner city and made money by selling items he found in garbage bins. He was HIV-positive and had suffered a heart attack only four months before the picture was taken. However, his life had not always been this way. Twenty years earlier, he was a chef on an oil rig, until he was involved in a head-on collision on his way home from work. After being in a coma for six months, he woke up with brain damage, which has made everyday tasks difficult ever since.

Tex could have cashed in on that trip and improved his own life, but he chose to give it away to better the lives of others instead. The cascade of kindness and generosity from all those who came together to make

Expressions of Humanity possible: this is what I remember most about my time working on the project.

Driven by my values of community, contribution, and creativity, along with my passion for photography and my skills for project management and team building, I set out to accomplish something that might bring meaning and value to the world. I achieved more than I dreamed I could and, in bringing the Expressions of Humanity project to life, I ignited new life in me, too. Although I didn't know it yet, for the first time in my life, I was experiencing the power that comes when working in harmony with the four principles laid out in the first half of this book: values, passion, skills, and service.

I can't wait for you to experience it, too.

PART TWO

HIT THE ROAD

WEEK 5

VISION AND GOALS: CREATING YOUR ROADMAP

The future depends on what you do today.
– MAHATMA GANDHI

Be careful, you might get exactly what you wish for.
– INDIANA JONES*

YOU ARE NOW EQUIPPED AND ON YOUR WAY ALONG THE ROAD TO change. Part Two will build on how to apply the four principles, with practical strategies for creating the change you want to see in the world. You'll learn ways to conceptualize and articulate your vision and goals, engage others to help you make them real, and overcome any obstacles that stand in the way. I'll also give you tips and tools for boosting your inner reserves, so you can stay on course over the long run.

Let's get started.

*Indiana Jones and the Kingdom of the Crystal Skull (2008)

A few years ago, I met Meredith Brown in her third-floor office off a busy street in the west end of Ottawa. After some small talk, she handed me a business card. On it, below her name, stood a word set in blue italics: *Riverkeeper*.

"How exactly do you *keep* a river?" I asked, settling into the seat across from her desk, curious to hear more.

"It is a bit of a daunting job title," Meredith confessed, "but I am honored by it."

Her task is formidable, given the sheer size of the Ottawa River system. From its headwaters in the Laurentian Mountains of central Quebec, the river runs over 750 miles, before draining into the St. Lawrence River at Montreal. Its watershed is more than 54,000 square miles—the size of the entire country of Bangladesh.

Only a few short years before Meredith was hired as the leader of the Ottawa Riverkeeper organization (a member of an international alliance), there was no official body looking after the health of the Ottawa River. Raw, untreated sewage was being dumped into the waterway on a frequent basis—the very place where numerous municipalities were drawing their drinking water from, people were swimming in, and wildlife depended on for existence. Meredith was determined to find out why this was happening. "Water is life," she told me passionately. "There isn't anything more important."

Meredith, an engineer with a degree in Resource and Environmental Management and substantial experience in watershed assessment and stream restoration, was steeped in the science of water. But she knew it would take more than that to save the river. "Resource management is about people management," she shared. For her, the position was a golden opportunity to work toward her vision, which was about advocacy and connecting with communities. "I wanted to be more proactive in how we can take care of our watersheds and avoid having to 'restore' our natural systems." When ecology is properly cared for by those who live in that ecosystem and depend on it, then restoration is not necessary.

She began as a one-person team but quickly began building a community of volunteers and supporters. "Fast-forward twelve years, and I now have eight staff and hundreds of volunteers who help us." There are lots of folks ready, willing, and able to involve themselves in the important ongoing cause of keeping the waterway healthy.

Now, thanks to their efforts, all levels of government (municipal, provincial, and federal) have come together to fund the Ottawa River Action Plan to reduce water pollution from combined sewer spills. As of today, the City of Ottawa has reduced the amount of untreated sewage going into the river by over 80 percent.

I asked Meredith what advice she would give to others who want to make a positive contribution to their communities. "Never lose sight of your vision, and find a compelling way to articulate it," she told me. Meredith is able to articulate her vision very clearly: "...a healthy Ottawa River that provides swimmable, drinkable, and fishable water for current and future generations, and is an inspiring model to the world." It is this clarity that inspired others to take up her vision as their own and join her in making a difference.

Most people want to engage in opportunities that are meaningful and make a difference, but many don't know how. If you, like Meredith, can articulate a compelling vision and offer a practical way to get involved, you are offering something of real value to people. "The Ottawa community has awakened to the beauty and importance of the river," she told me. "With solid and positive leadership, I'm convinced we can do just about anything."

Is Your Vision Clear?

Up to this point in the book, we've discussed four principles for living a life of purpose. They help to guide us on *how to be*, but they do not dictate what we *should do* with our lives.

If you're lucky enough to have adequate access to education and resources, there are an almost unlimited number of things you can do over the span of a lifetime. This knowledge is exhilarating, but also intimidating. It's easy to feel a bit lost and uncertain about which path to choose.

It might help to think of your life as a map. It begins blank, and over the years, you chart the course that marks your life's path. The thing is, you only have one map. Rather than filling it haphazardly as you go, hoping that you will eventually arrive at an interesting destination, why not determine where you want to go and plan how you'll get there first?

Here's where having a vision can help. Think of your vision as your final destination. A clear vision will provide direction to all facets of your life and help keep you on course as you navigate your grand adventure. This is what visionaries like Nelson Mandela, Oprah Winfrey, and Richard Branson accomplished on a grand scale—and you can do it for your own life, too. Realizing that you are the navigator of your own future is a powerful way to live. The question is, where do you want to go?

Meredith Brown has a vision for a healthy river system. On a larger scale, Gandhi had a vision for a democratic, united, and equitable India. Both examples, although obviously on different scales, are far-reaching and aspirational, and they require many people to make them real.

Some readers might want to aim high with a vision that impacts many people. Some of you won't. Perhaps your life aspirations look more like something Indiana Jones could really get behind—you want to follow your curiosity, have some great adventures, live an interesting life, and look dashing while you do it. Guess what? That's okay, too. It's more than likely, however, that you'll land somewhere between. What matters is that your vision is aspirational and true to you. Having an inspiring vision for yourself will keep you moving ahead in a positive direction, and your inner changes will ripple inevitably outward, even if it's just in small ways.

If your vision is not yet clear to you, don't worry; everyone is on their own unique life path, traveling at their own pace. Getting started is the important part. I will walk you through some exercises at the end of this week's chapter to help you to clarify your vision, but the formula is quite simple:

1. Dream (big)
2. Take action

It might take some time—years, even—but the journey is just as important as the destination, as you will continue to learn more about your values, discover new passions, and develop your skills. All of this will serve to both clarify your vision and bring you closer to your destination.

I Have a Dream

What makes for a compelling vision—one that sparks your passion and draws you out to be the change you want to see in the world, as well as inspiring others to do the same? To answer this question, let's consider one of the most celebrated speeches of the twentieth century.

On August 28, 1963, American civil rights leader Martin Luther King Jr. addressed a crowd of over 250,000 people from the steps of the Lincoln Memorial in Washington, DC. In a speech that lasted just over sixteen minutes, King eloquently shared his vision of an end to racial segregation and discrimination in the United States.

"I have a dream that my four little children will one day live in a nation where they will not be judged by the color of their skin, but by the content of their character," he proclaimed.

Notice three things about this iconic line.

First, it is plainspoken. King does not use complex terminology or technical jargon to describe his vision for the future. He uses simple and concrete language to depict a fair and just future, where his own children are judged by what they contribute to the world rather than how they are perceived in it. Anyone can relate to this vision; its simplicity makes it powerful.

Second, it provides a positive, hopeful outlook. His words depict a future worth fighting for—one that inspires others to join him and take action to make his vision a reality.

Third, he links to the essence of what matters to him most: his children. He doesn't talk about principles and ideas; he focuses on why his dream matters. By doing this, he unlocks listeners' abilities to do the same. They are not moved by the logic of his idea, but because it aligns with their values and connects with their heart. The dream becomes larger, shared, belonging to many.

Martin Luther King Jr. had a clear vision and found a compelling way to communicate it to others. This helped him to engage others and recruit them in bringing his vision to life. You don't need to be an orator or world-famous activist like Martin Luther King Jr. to emulate his example. To change the world—even if it's just your small corner of it—first, imagine the future you want to achieve, then find a way to articulate your vision so it will connect authentically with the hearts and minds of others. It may just inspire them to join you in making that future a reality.

Landmarks on Your Roadmap

Once you have a clear vision, how do you start making it real? As I have said, the next phase is about action. But how, and when, should you act? You'll figure this out by setting goals and breaking your aspirations down into smaller chunks that are more concrete, realistic, and faster to accomplish than the entirety of your vision.

It may be helpful to think of your vision and goals collectively as a roadmap for your future. Vision is the destination, and goals are the landmarks, which help you navigate and plot your route on the map. You could have the best map in the world, super accurate and detailed, but if it's not taking you where you want to go, then it's not really much help. So, you need to know where you're going first, and that means having a clear vision. Conversely, even if you are very clear about where you want to go, you probably won't get there without a good map, and that's why concrete goals are so important.

Goals provide milestones throughout your journey. They keep you on course, help you to mark your progress, and give you something to work toward on the road ahead. However, not all goals are created equal.

GET SPECIFIC

Have you ever made a New Year's resolution, only to give it up a few weeks later? If so, don't worry—you are far from alone. According to research from the University of Scranton in Pennsylvania, an estimated 92 percent of people who make a New Year's resolution fail to realize their goal. This raises a question: What is it that the other 8 percent do right?

Year after year, my garden-variety resolutions to exercise more, or drink less, would wither long before the start of spring. However, one year, despite my poor track record, I found myself among the elite 8 percent who succeed. That year, my resolution was to read twenty new books by year's end—a target I surpassed by mid-September. What had I done right this time, when so many past attempts had failed?

In the book *Switch*, Chip and Dan Heath discuss the best ways to make a change in behavior stick. Let's say you want to start eating a healthier diet, so you make a goal to "eat healthier." Despite your best intentions, you fall back into your old ways a mere two weeks later. Sound familiar? According to the Heath brothers, the main reason for faltering isn't laziness. It's a lack of clarity. Your objective to "eat healthier" is just too sweeping and ambiguous to execute in your day-to-day life. Ambiguity, it turns out, is why many of us fail to reach our goals.

Your chances of success will be much greater if you make a goal that provides clear direction: something that leaves no wiggle room for digression. For example, you're more likely to create a lasting change in your eating habits if you aim to change one specific behavior, such as switching from whole milk to skim milk, rather than trying to overhaul all your eating habits in one fell swoop. A goal like "Only drink skim milk" works because it's laser-focused, unambiguous, and easy to follow.

This helps to explain why I was able to achieve my goal of reading twenty new books in a year. What I didn't do was make a vague resolution to "read more" in the new year; instead, I was specific about the number of books I'd read and the time frame in which I'd read them.

Originally, I thought twenty books in a year would be a stretch—doable, but ambitious. However, as is often the case with big goals, they can seem less overwhelming if you break them down into bite-size chunks. To read this many books in one year means finishing a book every two and a half weeks, on average. That works out to reading twenty pages a day, assuming a typical book has roughly 350 pages. Now that's workable. In retrospect, my resolution wasn't so far-fetched after all. Just by reading a little every day, I was able to reach my target before the start of fall.

You can use concrete short-term goals as steps on your way to reaching much higher aspirations. After I completed my New Year's resolution, I did in fact create a longer-term goal to read at least one hundred books in four years. It took three years and 301 days to complete this goal. Ahead of schedule—hurrah! And I was so encouraged by the outcome that I ratcheted up my use of goal setting in personal and professional areas.

Specific, measurable goals help you to focus your energy and efforts on achieving the things you want out of life, and when directed toward your vision, goals can help you convert your blue-sky aspirations into concrete stages. When you complete one goal after another, you will travel step-by-step toward your ultimate destination. And one day, it's very possible that you will have realized your vision.

Advanced Goal Setting

Seeing all your goals set on paper can be daunting—another laundry list of things to do in an already busy life. For many people, this can lead to a sense of overwhelm, or even paralysis. However, it's important to understand that this is a process, which can be broken down into bite-size pieces that are manageable on a daily basis. By taking small, consistent steps, creating a strategy to support yourself, and adjusting that strategy along the way, you'll keep moving ahead to becoming the change you want to see. You may reach the finish line with some goals before you know it. Others may require more time, and some may never be met. That is normal, and it is perfectly okay. The important thing is to stay on the journey.

I suggest a four-step process for developing and completing your goals. It has worked for me and my students, and it can work for you, too.

STEP 1: CREATE YOUR GOALS

Words matter. In fact, how a goal is expressed in language can sometimes be the difference between accomplishing it and falling short. It certainly can affect our motivation. So, think about how your choice of language reflects what you are aiming for.

Consider the aptly named S.M.A.R.T. criteria when you are creating your goals. The five criteria are often defined as:

Specific: A goal like "Increase search engine traffic on my website by 10 percent in the next quarter" is more concrete than "Boost website traffic."

Measurable: You need to be able to measure progress and know when the goal has been reached. "Educate school children about bullying" is not easily measurable, but "Teach a bullying seminar at North Park School next month" is.

Attainable: It's good to push your limits, but important to focus on what you can achieve with your strengths. "Stop climate change" may be your ideal vision, but it's not an attainable goal for one person. Perhaps you're a good speaker with great people skills, in which case, "Start a vlog series on climate change by May and arrange for at least two experts to interview online" would be realistic.

Relevant: When aligned with your vision and values, a goal is naturally relevant to you. If you're passionate about clean oceans, for instance, then "Spend three hours picking up trash off the beach every weekend" is a good fit.

Time-bound: Give yourself a reasonable deadline that's not too short or long. "Learn how to sing opera by the end of the month" is probably not a reasonable deadline!

STEP 2: PLAN YOUR WORK

To quote the French writer and aviator Antoine de Saint-Exupéry, "A goal without a plan is just a wish." To accomplish your goals—especially the more involved ones—create a plan for achieving them. Your plan doesn't need to be long or complicated to be effective, as long as it has a clear timeline with actionable steps and milestones.

STEP 3: WORK YOUR PLAN

Once you've created your plan, don't file it away in a place you rarely look. For your plan to work, you must *work it*—refer to it often and revise it if necessary. And then, you need to take action; if not every day, then at least at regular intervals.

Your plan may involve teamwork with others. It's important to stay in communication and ensure you're all on the same page with your objectives and tasks, are working efficiently, sharing the load, and not letting anything or anyone fall through the cracks.

Even if you are working on a solo project, it can help to have someone to check in with. You know how having a workout buddy at the gym keeps you motivated? Do something similar here. Meet a friend over coffee regularly to check in about your respective goals. Share your objectives and obstacles. It's way more fun to celebrate your triumphs and laugh at your tribulations when your friends are around.

There may be times when you don't make progress, and even times when you may feel like giving up completely. When you hit a rough patch, try asking yourself: What's one small action I can take today to advance just one of my goals? It could be the tiniest thing imaginable: make a phone call, write a post on social media, or do some online research. Just keep moving forward.

STEP 4: LEARN FROM YOUR TRIALS

Accomplishment feels great. Celebrate! Still, you may very well fall short in achieving some of your goals. And you know what? That's just fine. It doesn't mean you're at fault, and it doesn't mean you have lost your vision. Don't forget the value of having a growth mindset; think of your goal-setting practice as an experiment, rather than an indication of your self-worth. Just like a good scientist, try to learn from your trials. Remember, all failure is feedback. Ask yourself: What changes can I make based on my experience? What would be the probable outcomes from making these changes? The bottom line is that not all experiments will be successful, but all of them can teach you something.

Achieving Your Vision: Think in Cycles

When planning for a big project, I have found that five years is a good timeline to start with. It is short enough to be reasonable and long enough to encapsulate all the goals I need to reach in order to create something really special.

With the Project Change university course, this included developing the syllabus, going through all the administrative hoops to get it approved, creating the curriculum and lesson plans, and teaching it a few times in order to iron out the kinks. It's fair to say it took around five years to get the course to the point where it stood on its own and was of good quality.

This same five-year principle held true when I decided to pursue my lifelong dream of starting a foundation that provides grants and resources to fledgling charities working to improve their communities. The Project Change Foundation took a year to develop and launch. Over the next few years, we learned a lot about the needs of early-stage charities and continued to refine our approach for supporting them. Our goal is to nurture financially sustainable, well-organized charities capable of standing the test of time—and of course, we also want this for the Project Change

Foundation itself. As our fund grows, so does our capacity to invest in more organizations in the future. We found our winning strategy.

It took about five years to build the foundation to the point where I could step away from it. At the time of writing this, the foundation is now in its sixth year. I am still actively involved and very much enjoying the work. I'm not considering walking away at this point, but if something were to change for me, the foundation would continue on just fine. The people involved are remarkable, and the systems are solid. The foundation truly has a life of its own, and that gives me a lot of satisfaction.

At the end of a five-year cycle, you may or may not want to step away, but the project should be at a point where it can stand on its own. Of course, five isn't a hard-and-fast rule. Some ideas will take less time to bring to life, while others will take more. For some people, five years might seem like a long stretch of time; for others, it's not enough. You might find you tend to operate on two-year cycles, or ten. Breaking it down helps you prioritize what you want to accomplish, and it can motivate you to get out there and make it happen.

To use my five-year example, let's say you are twenty years old and envisioning what you'd like to accomplish by the time you retire at seventy. In this scenario, you have ten five-year cycles ahead of you. Sure, fifty years is a long time, but ten is not a big number. That's more or less the number of large-scale projects you have time to pursue. Barring a scientific breakthrough in human longevity, you only have so many shots to realize your big ideas and create something special. Don't waste them.

There's a quote by productivity consultant and author David Allen, which goes: "You can do anything, but you can't do everything." Thinking in terms of discrete cycles helps to bring this point home. Your potential is almost unlimited, but the time available to make your mark is not. Don't let this thought scare you—use it to motivate you. Life is precious. Focus your time on the things that count, and tune out the things that don't.

Someday May Never Come

In 2014, when I traveled to Bali for my six-month sabbatical, I intended to start writing this book. I was making progress until my father's illness and sudden death changed my trajectory completely.

I was thrust into a time of deep reflection while I examined my past, thought about my future, and questioned what was really important to me. I realized that, although my teaching was rewarding, I still felt a lack of direction. I couldn't answer the question, *What kind of legacy do I want to leave?*

Up until that point, I hadn't given it much consideration. "I'll get to it someday," I'd tell myself. But now, the question mattered. Urgently. I understood that my life is precious, fragile, and fleeting, and that "someday" may never come.

I decided then that I needed to start on my legacy project *today*. Over the next several days, I created the exercises described at the end of this week's chapter, which in turn helped to shape the first draft of my vision statement. I then fleshed out the details for a major project that would advance my vision: to start the Project Change Foundation. I'd had the seed of this idea for some time, and I thought that it would be something I could do to honor my dad who, as I mentioned earlier, was a man who used his actions to help others.

I knew this project wasn't something I could do alone, so I enlisted some friends and colleagues whom I admired greatly and whose mix of talents I thought would benefit the foundation. I asked them if they'd join me as founding board members and was surprised when they all agreed. In 2015, the Project Change Foundation was officially registered as a Canadian charity, and to date we've supported seven budding nonprofits in their development. You never know where an idea might go until you release it into the world. My father never got to see the Project Change Foundation, but I know he'd be proud.

Confronting mortality, whether in a loved one or yourself, can be a powerful motivator to get moving on a meaningful project. Just as my dad's death inspired me to take action on my foundation, Steve Jobs found that his own impending death helped him double down on living in accordance with his own values.

In 2005, the year after he was diagnosed with cancer, the CEO and cofounder of Apple gave a moving commencement speech to the graduating class at Stanford University. In the speech, Jobs urged the newly graduated students to do what they love and to never lose sight of their dreams. Reflecting on his cancer diagnosis, Jobs suggested that awareness of your own death can be a motivator for doing what's truly important in your life: "Remembering that I'll be dead soon is the most important tool I've ever encountered to help me make the big choices in life. Because almost everything—all external expectations, all pride, all fear of embarrassment or failure—these things just fall away in the face of death, leaving only what is truly important. Remembering that you are going to die is the best way I know to avoid the trap of thinking you have something to lose. You are already naked. There is no reason not to follow your heart."

Contemplating death and the ephemeral nature of life can give you the courage to overcome procrastination and any fear that's holding you back. Say, for example, you're a writer with an inspirational story to share. You want to do this in front of an audience, but you're afraid of public speaking. What's the worst that can happen? You get a frog in your throat? Sweat buckets? Freeze up? Feel embarrassed?...So what? It really doesn't matter. Trust me, when you're dead and buried in one hundred years, no one is going to remember or care. Like life itself, fear is ephemeral.

Here's the silver lining: Embracing the impermanence of life can free you to go after your dreams. If you want to run your own business, start that plan. If you want to make beautiful art, do it. If you want to volunteer overseas, buy your ticket now. Don't let fear or other people's opinions stop you. Don't let the risk of failure stop you. Those are just temporary hurdles in the grand scheme of things. When fear falls away, anything is possible. Go for it—follow your heart and begin living your dreams.

Remember, Martin Luther King Jr. didn't live long enough to see his dream realized, but it didn't die with him. It lived on in the hearts of those who took up his vision and is still being moved forward to this day. A strong vision with clear goals can harness the power of the collective, and it has the potential to change not only your life, but the lives of others around you. If you're lucky, it will live on as a legacy that continues to be the change you wished to see in the world.

Week 5 Lesson Summary

- Your vision is your ultimate destination: the future as you want to see it. Goals are your landmarks. They keep you on track and moving ahead toward the change you want to see in the world.
- Realize that you are the navigator of your own journey. Rather than letting life happen arbitrarily, be an active participant in bringing your chosen vision to the world.
- Articulate your vision—write it down and share it with others. Follow the example of Martin Luther King Jr. and use language that is simple and heartfelt. The right choice of words can be incredibly motivating, for you and for others.
- Goals provide direction as you steer toward your long-term vision. Set yourself up for success by creating targets that are clear and concrete.
- Create a strategy that can be adjusted as you go. Small, consistent steps will add up to big changes over time.
- It often takes years to take a big idea from concept to fruition. A good rule of thumb is to plan in terms of five-year cycles.
- Don't let fear stop you from pursuing your dreams. Like life itself, fear is transitory. This might seem counterintuitive, but embracing the impermanence of life can release you from the grip of fear. Once you've let go, anything might be possible— even your wildest aspirations.

Week 5 Exercises

1. DREAM BIG

Remember the formula for making your vision a reality? 1) Dream big. 2) Take action. We're going to start with dreaming big!

Imagine yourself at a ripe old age and nearing the end of your life. You've lived a good and fulfilling life. You've stayed true to yourself, nurtured your passions, and pursued your dreams. Fear has not stopped you from doing what's important. You've lived a life to be proud of—one that has brought you much happiness and a deep sense of meaning. Now, thinking back over the entire course of your life, answer these questions:

What have you created or done? What difference have you made to others? What positive footprints have you left behind? Consider different areas: family, relationships, professional, service, spiritual, etc.

2. CRAFT YOUR VISION

You're now going to take a crack at writing down your vision for the future you wish to create. Write a statement that encompasses your imagined future. In just a few short sentences, try to capture the essence of what you see in your mind. Use concrete words and phrases, like Meredith Brown does when talking about the river ("swimmable, drinkable, and fishable water for current and future generations").

Articulating a vision can be challenging, and it might take several tries to have it land right for you. Get creative and experiment with different language. One place to start is to finish this sentence: "My vision for a better world is…"

Don't worry if you don't land on the perfect vision statement. You can always revise it later. If you're having difficulty, try switching to another medium, and try drawing or collaging.

3. THINK IN CYCLES

Imagine your life in five years. To be on track with your long-term vision, what should your life look like? What are your successes? Ask yourself: What do I want to create? What impact do I want to make? What will my legacy be? Brainstorm one big project you could do in the next five years that would help move your vision forward.

4. GET S.M.A.R.T.

Imagine yourself working on this five-year project. To be on pace, where should you be at this time next year? What accomplishments have you ticked off the list? Now, create two or three concrete goals for the next year that will keep you lined up for success. Use the S.M.A.R.T. criteria to ensure your goals are effectively stated. Remember, these goals are meant to get you closer to realizing your grand vision. You should feel compelled to complete them, even if they are ambitious.

5. GET GOING

Now, come back to the present moment. What's one thing you can do today to help create this future? What can you do by midnight today to put you on track to reach those goals? Write it down.

Weekly Challenge: Take Action

This week's challenge is to spend at least thirty minutes each day taking action on your vision and goals.

Congratulations! You've done the work of dreaming big and, hopefully, come up with some goals for moving your vision forward. Now you get to take action.

If you completed the exercises above, you already have identified an action you can take today to advance your goals. Now, go ahead and plan an action for every day this week.

Try not to set your expectations too high—most likely, you'll hardly scratch the surface of your long-term vision. The point of this challenge is not to achieve your vision outright but to get into the habit of acting on it. The idea is to become the type of person who pursues one's dreams, rather than just fantasizing.

Set aside a block of time every day to do things from your list. Rather than focusing on a single big task that you probably won't finish in one week, I recommend doing several smaller activities. Make sure you can complete these tasks within the week. That way, you can enjoy the feeling of accomplishment that comes from checking things off your to-do list. Now, get out there and chart your course to a better future.

Don't forget to journal about your experiences with this weekly challenge before moving on to Week 6. For more direction, refer to the guide for self-reflection in the Appendix.

WEEK 6

COMMUNITY CONNECTIONS: BUILDING BRIDGES

A small body of determined spirits fired by an unquenchable faith in their mission can alter the course of history.
– MAHATMA GANDHI

Well, you know me, always glad to help.
– INDIANA JONES*

IN 2010, MICHAEL SCHRATTER TOOK A LEAVE OF ABSENCE FROM his job as a Vancouver schoolteacher, moved his worldly possessions into storage, said goodbye to his family and friends, and set off on one heck of a bicycle ride.

Over the next year and a half, Michael would ride his Norco Cabot the distance of the earth's circumference at the equator—nearly 25,000 miles. Loaded down with 106 pounds of gear and supplies, he

Indiana Jones and the Kingdom of the Crystal Skull (2008)

cycled through thirty-three countries on six continents, before returning home to Vancouver 469 days later.

This Homeric odyssey was much more than a supersized adventure. The trip was fueled by a highly personal cause. Driven by his experiences with bipolar disorder and the shame and confusion associated with it, Michael used his global tour to draw attention to the stigma surrounding mental illness. He called his journey Ride Don't Hide.

"Until quite recently, mental illness was viewed very negatively," Michael said, referring to the all-too-common perception of people with mental illness as unstable or dangerous. "This is a false portrayal. Most people who deal with a mental illness are productive, competent, well-balanced individuals who have careers, families, and friends. Unfortunately, most of them stay silent about their condition, as they don't want to be associated with the powerfully destructive portrayal of mental illness. It is not until they choose to stop hiding and come into view that the accurate story of mental illness can be revealed, and the stigma dissolved."

Ride Don't Hide was so successful that it became an annual fundraising effort in communities across the country and is now Canada's largest annual participatory mental health awareness event. How did one person's dream morph into something so huge? By engaging others.

"In my opinion, no matter how passionate and intelligent you might be, it is imperative to realize that you can't build your vision by yourself. There simply isn't enough time in the day. Not to mention, there are others who are more talented than you at certain tasks that need to get done."

Every day, you interact with a wide range of people from different circles: family, friends, neighbors, coworkers, acquaintances, and even strangers. These people can be a tremendous source of support and a valuable resource as you work toward your goals. Getting their help, however, is not always easy, so we need to learn how to build bridges sometimes. And it should come as no surprise that there are different methods of bridge-building for different types of relationships.

Nurture Your Strong and Weak Ties

The people within your own community possess an abundant wealth of resources. Tapping into these resources will greatly enhance your success. But before you go out there asking for help, make sure your connections are as broad and as strong as possible. You must invest time and energy in cultivating and strengthening relationships—inside and outside your immediate networks—first. This requires a deliberate and consistent practice, and a mindset of giving back.

The word "community" here simply means a group of interconnected people who share common characteristics, goals, or interests. Residents of a neighborhood or town comprise a community, but so do people who work at the same company, go to the same school, attend the same church, or belong to the same social network. One of my communities, for example, is the university where I teach. It's an extensive network of over eight thousand students, almost a thousand faculty and staff, and countless alumni, donors, and others who are connected with the university. There's a good chance that you belong to several different communities—and they can also overlap; coworkers can be part of the same social circle, neighbors can go to the same temple, and school peers can play on the same sports team. The communities you belong to may shift over time as your interests and priorities change across different stages of life, but no matter where you are, community ties are vital.

Broadly, your community connections can be categorized as either strong or weak ties. Strong ties can include family, friends, and affiliations with neighbors, coworkers, etc. Proximity sets the stage for strong ties to form, but this can take time. You may be keen on jumping ahead and asking your colleague or your neighbor to join in on your kid's school fundraising effort, but it's better to exercise some patience and good judgment. Requests for support within your strong ties are usually reciprocated at some point, so make sure you're responding to their asks as well. This isn't just about your great cause. Nobody likes to feel as if they're being taken advantage of.

Weak ties are all the broader connections within your communities, and your familiarity with these people will vary. Some you may know moderately well (a cousin, your dentist, or a friend's buddy), but others you may only associate with casually (a store clerk, librarian, or postal carrier). Reinforcing these ties is important because it expands the reach of your network, but at the same time, it may also reveal the potential for deeper connections.

Strengthening your weak ties takes time—so, take the time. Most people appreciate giving and receiving small gestures, so begin by remarking on the little things you notice or are curious about. Do you admire your new neighbor's garden? Tell him so. Did your favorite barista mention going to the local farmers' market? You can share a recipe using in-season produce with them. The value of small talk is vastly underrated. It lays the foundation for connecting at a deeper level, where we find our shared values and ultimately come together to create a better world. The next time you find yourself thinking that small talk is a waste of time, why not make a game of it? Give yourself the challenge of finding three things you have in common with the person you are talking to. You'd be surprised how easy it is to find common ground, even with someone who seems like your total opposite.

Take this attitude into your relationships, and then start to expand and strengthen the connections in all areas of your life. Don't forget, you can also begin forming new connections with people you don't know. Take an interactive class at a community center, join a Meetup group that interests you and attend one of their events, shop at a locally owned business and strike up a conversation with the shopkeeper, or simply be intentional about smiling and saying hello to passersby on the street. If the thought of meeting new people makes you nervous, consider that, except for your parents and siblings, all the strong ties in your life were once weak ties, and before that, they were not connections at all. Even your best friend was once a stranger.

Here's a quick example to illustrate the importance of weak ties. In the summer of 2015, I traveled coast-to-coast from Vancouver to Halifax in search of ordinary people who were doing something remarkable to effect positive change. I called it The Better World Tour. Many of the people featured in this book were those I interviewed on this trip.

The four-week journey took me to eleven different cities. Since I didn't have strong connections in many of the places that I visited, I leveraged the power of my weak ties on social media to discover and connect with these change-makers. It's not a stretch to say that the tour (and perhaps even this book) wouldn't have been possible without the recommendations and connections provided by my weak ties—proving that "weak ties" are not synonymous with weak relationships, or weak impact. I'll forever remember the kindness, enthusiasm, and generosity of the folks I met on the trip, and their role in bringing my own vision to reality.

Good for You, Good for All

Growing up on the outskirts of a small town, the importance of home security was never really instilled in me as a kid. Our front door was almost always unlocked. Perhaps we owned little of value, but I think it had more to do with the small-town sense of community.

Our family had strong ties with our neighbors, so we didn't worry about break-ins. And, it turns out, this lack of concern was well founded; research shows that a neighborhood's collective efficacy (a fusion of social trust, a sense of engagement, ownership of public space, and a shared willingness to intervene) correlates with lower violent-crime rates. Social cohesion equals more safety.

More recently, I have lived in a three-story apartment building in Vancouver. I locked my door even when at home. Although I was polite to my neighbors, the social bonds between us were weak at best, even after many years. Shrouded in an air of aloofness, the city can feel downright lonely at times. The same can be said for many cities across the world, and countless studies show that city-dwellers find it difficult to make friends or even ask for help from those who live nearby yet remain nameless.

Urbanization is on the rise. The majority of people now live in cities. Despite it being more difficult to create a sense of neighborhood and community within a city, there is ample evidence that it is well worth our efforts to try.

When social ties are secure, we feel less isolated and have a more deeply felt sense of belonging, which is better for our mental health. It also gives us more incentive to get involved. We're more likely to volunteer; vote; participate in neighborhood events; give input on community issues; and support local business, arts, and culture. This so-called social capital has also been shown, through economic statistics, to drive innovation, entrepreneurship, and economic growth.

A cohesive community is also well equipped to manage problems and adapt to adversity, whether these are ongoing issues such as poverty or sudden emergencies like a natural disaster. When connections are robust, we can more effectively act as a team when responding to problems and gathering resources. Conversely, when we show up for each other during a crisis, this also strengthens our social bonds. We saw numerous examples of this during the COVID-19 pandemic. The collective sense that "we are in this together" had a powerful influence in strengthening a sense of common identity and cohesion within urban communities.

The other advantage to building community within a city is the greater diversity within the population. Evidence shows that the more diverse our group, the broader our scope of creative thinking and problem solving is. This is a classic case of the whole being greater than the sum of its parts.

Ultimately, whether rural or urban, building bridges in your community creates a healthier, more vibrant, more engaged place to live for all.

Ask What You Can Do...

Margaret Stacey has a long history in the arts and theater community in Nelson, British Columbia—a small town in the Selkirk Mountains, an eight-hour drive east of Vancouver. She's retired now, but for seventeen years, Margaret managed the historic Capitol Theatre, a beautifully

restored 426-seat gem that, over the years, has hosted a catalog of theatrical productions from *Annie* to *West Side Story*. Her work then, and
later on as a two-term city councillor, has had an immeasurable impact
on the town's art scene. However, I wasn't in Nelson to talk with Margaret about her professional life. I was there to ask her what she does in
her downtime.

For the thirty-plus years that Margaret has lived in Nelson, she has
been creating large art installations. "I like big canvases, Coroplast, ply-
wood, set flats or bare walls, long rolls of paper, house exteriors, big cut
outs, photo stand-ins," she told me. "Small blank pages intimidate me."

The scale of her work is impressive, but what's remarkable is that she
has given most of her artwork to the community. Her pieces—ranging
from wall-sized murals to theatrical set pieces to eight-foot-tall poster
art—have all been donated to local churches, theaters, schools, and other
organizations.

What has inspired Margaret to keep giving her time and creativity for
all these years? She explained that, everywhere she has lived—and despite
not knowing if she'd be there for one year or thirty—she fully committed to both the place and its people. "I have always thought that human
engagement was the most important part of the process."

Margaret took me on an impromptu trip around town to show me
some of her artwork. We stopped in the alleyway behind the Capitol Theatre to view the murals that cover its back wall. Back in 1990, the place
was in rough condition, she told me. But she had a vision. "We just started
from a small corner, and it expanded all over the back and side of the
building, as far as we could reach. And this still continues today." Standing there, I asked Margaret what she would identify as the biggest lesson
gleaned from all her years of giving back to the community. "If a person
has skills of any kind, there's always a way to use them, wake them up, try
them out, hone them in some way to animate the surrounding sphere of
influence," she explained.

Margaret's philosophy made me think of the famous quote by John
F. Kennedy (JFK): "Ask not what your country can do for you; ask what

you can do for your country." People who view their communities only in terms of the resources they provide will not get very far in building connections. We all know people who only show up in your life when they want something from you. Annoying, right? You feel that you've been taken advantage of, and trust erodes. While their actions might sting you, the harm those people cause themselves is much greater. They might benefit in the short term, but the tarnished relationships and damage to their reputation will hurt them in the long run.

Conduct an honest assessment of your own interactions with people in your communities. If you give more than you take, then pat yourself on the back and keep doing what you're doing. But, if you take more than you give, it's time to shift the balance. Be sure to congratulate yourself for your honesty. It takes a mature person to own their shortcomings. And it's not too late—there's still time to break old patterns and form better habits.

We have a chance to redeem ourselves every day. Every morning, we have a decision to make. Do we live the day just for ourselves, or for others as well, by serving our communities? This doesn't mean you need to live like a monk. It's still important to care for yourself and enjoy your life, but long-term happiness and fulfillment come from nurturing connections with others. That's the whole point—what's good for others is good for you, too.

In 1938, the Harvard Study of Adult Development began tracking 724 men, analyzing things like blood samples, brain scans (once they became available), and self-reported surveys. (Coincidentally, JFK was one of the original participants.) The study has continued over the past eighty years—one of the longest studies of its kind—and its findings revealed that the number-one key to living a fulfilling life is not money or fame. It's not the type of work you do or the model of car you drive. The most significant contributing factor to your quality of life is the quality of your relationships.

The study found that participants who had good relationships with family, friends, and community were more likely to have lived flourishing lives than those with weaker bonds. According to Robert Waldinger, the director of the study, "It turns out that people who are more socially con-nected to family, to friends, to community, are happier. They're physically healthier, and they live longer than people who are less well-connected." In fact, the quality of our relationships is a better predictor of living a long and happy life than social class, intelligence, or even genes. That certainly proved to be true for Margaret. When I asked her about the biggest ben-efits she saw from her community art projects, she told me: "One makes surprising friends, stays engaged, possibly lives longer, continues to learn and grow, and leaves a legacy."

Abide by JFK's call to action: Ask yourself what you can do for your neighbors, your community, and your world, then do it. On the surface, this seems like a call for self-sacrifice. But upon deeper reflection, we can see that living this way isn't solely about selflessness. Far from it. When you actively serve your communities, you build up your social connec-tions. Bolstering these ties means you are doing the single most important thing you can do to make your life healthier, happier, and fuller. Are you surprised? This is the Gandhiana Jones Project, after all.

Engaging Hearts and Minds

Michael Redhead Champagne (aka the North End MC) is an expert on community engagement. Michael is an Indigenous Canadian activist from the Cree Nation, born and raised in Winnipeg's North End. Grow-ing up, he witnessed firsthand the influence of gangs on youth in his inner-city neighborhood, and at the age of twenty-three, he decided to do something about it.

In 2010, Michael created AYO! Aboriginal Youth Opportunities, an "anti-gang" whose goal is encouraging Indigenous youth to embrace their unique gifts, in order to create new opportunities in the community. "Our beginnings as an anti-gang are rooted in the fact that gangs were highly effective at attracting teenagers in our community," Michael explained to me, while we chatted at a cafeteria on the campus of the University of Winnipeg. "We recognized that if we wanted to engage young people as successfully as street gangs, we needed to replace the allure of crime with something more attractive. That something else was an opportunity to be a leader, a student, and to have a place to belong—a family."

Early on, Michael recognized the importance of collaboration. But how do you get people involved in building your vision when it's still a glimmer in your mind's eye? Champagne found his solution in the traditional teachings on the Medicine Wheel, which has been part of Indigenous cultures for thousands of years. His approach harnesses the four dimensions of the Wheel—Spirit, Body, Heart, and Mind—as guideposts for how to engage people and benefit from their knowledge and skills at each step of developing his project.

The first dimension of the Medicine Wheel, he said, is Spirit. "In the early stages, share your idea with those who will nurture, support, and care for it," Michael said, describing the fragile and fluid nature of Spirit. He stressed the importance of finding people who share your vision. This can include your family, friends, or anyone else. "Seek out people who, like you, believe the world needs the idea. These safe conversations will teach you how to express the true spirit of your idea with others." For our purposes, the point of these early explorative conversations is to clarify the essential core of your idea, build your confidence in it, and generate momentum to get it off the ground.

Next, Michael described the second dimension of the Medicine Wheel, which is Body, in relation to his work. Once you've captured the Spirit of your idea, he told me, the next step is to start making it real and give it Body. Write about your goals, approach, and expected benefits of your project. Then share your proposal with a wide range of people and solicit feedback from those whose opinion you value. An idea in its infancy is delicate, so don't let it—or you—get crushed by criticism. "People may disagree with parts of your idea, so be ready to be challenged," Michael cautioned. "Don't take it personally."

Once you've sculpted the Body of your idea, Michael told me, you must discover its Heart: the Medicine Wheel's third dimension. "This is where you learn to express the emotional reasons for moving your idea forward," Michael advised. Imagine you have an upcoming meeting to pitch a big idea to a potential investor, partner, or customer. It doesn't matter how great it is; if you cannot get your audience to care about your idea, it will be difficult to gain their attention and support—and how you get them to care is by connecting through an emotional narrative. Keep in mind that most people tend to care more about other people than about facts and figures, so talk about what impact you hope your project will have on real lives. Find the story in your vision. Stories are powerful tools to engage others on an emotional level, especially when you can tell one from your own life.

The fourth and final aspect of the Medicine Wheel is Mind. Once you've engaged others' hearts, it's time to connect with their intellect. The human mind likes reasons, rationality, and practicality. Avoid using generic, fuzzy language when describing your plans and requirements for getting your project off the ground. Strive to be clear and concrete, and use examples to help paint a picture. While you don't want to bore people with too much detail, mentioning one or two key statistics or the results from an important study can support your idea's credibility. You may also want to consider highlighting your affiliation with a highly regarded person or organization, if applicable, for instant legitimacy through association. Make sure that they approve of this, either implicitly or explicitly, that your connection is genuine, and that the respect goes both ways. Then it's a win-win.

To me, Michael Redhead Champagne's approach stressed the importance of engaging different people in different ways throughout the stages of bringing vision to life, and how important it is to engage both hearts and minds when building something new with others. Near the end of our interview, I asked Michael to reflect on the most valuable lesson he has learned through his work as a community builder. Taking a moment to contemplate, he eloquently observed, "A single strand of sweetgrass is weak, but many strands together in a braid is strong."

Marketing 101

Knowing *when* and *who* we should turn to at various stages of our work is one thing; knowing *how* to engage people and ask for their help is quite another.

Let's say one of your goals is to raise $10,000 for your favorite charity, and you decide to put on a fundraising event. If you've ever been involved in event planning, you know that a big part of the job is signing people up, from attendees to volunteers and sponsors. How you communicate your request matters, and this was one of the areas where my students struggled the most. It turns out, some simple skills pulled directly from the world of marketing proved tremendously helpful.

Simon Sinek, an inspirational speaker and the author of multiple books, including *Start with Why*, investigates the ways we affect each other. We can either manipulate or inspire, he says, but the latter is far more powerful. "People don't buy *what* you do. They buy *why* you do it." In his TED Talk, Sinek explains how this response is grounded in biology. Our limbic system is responsible for our feelings and our gut-level reactions, and most people make decisions that are highly influenced by this "emotional brain." Explaining the features of something (the *what*) on a rational level is not likely to persuade us, but heartfelt sharing is. Simon uses Apple's marketing communication to provide an example.

"If Apple were like everyone else, a marketing message from them might sound like this: 'We make great computers. They're beautifully designed, simple to use, and user friendly. Wanna buy one?'...It's uninspiring. Here's how Apple actually communicates: 'In everything we do, we believe in challenging the status quo. We believe in thinking differently. The way we challenge the status quo is by making our products beautifully designed, simple to use, and user friendly. We just happen to make great computers. Wanna buy one?'"

If you can clearly communicate on an emotional level the *why* of your vision, you will attract others with whom it resonates. And this means they will be more likely to join your venture.

Once you have attracted the right people, you do need to talk about the *what*. In sales lingo, this is known as "the pitch," and it can often come off sounding disingenuous. This is partly because most of us tend to describe the features of the thing we're offering, instead of how it (whether an object, idea, or experience) will affect others. Sometimes, people need to know that their participation can benefit them on a personal level. So, frame your project as an opportunity, and be ready to answer the question, "What's in it for me?"

When teaching my Project Change course, I developed an activity to help students practice this skill. I would show the students a beautiful gold meditation bowl that I use regularly in class, telling them to imagine that each of them is the proud owner of a shop that sells these sorts of bowls. Then I announce that I'm a customer who has just walked through their shop door, intrigued by what was on display in the window when I happened to pass it.

Approaching a few students in turn, I will say, "Sell me this bowl." Most of them talk about the features of the bowl, describing its visual and auditory qualities, like the fact that it's gold in color, and that you can make it ring or "sing" by tapping it in the right way. Typically, only a few students highlight the benefits of the bowl, like its soothing sound and the fact that it can help you relax. It is only the rare student, one who has truly grasped the concept of good marketing, who will think to describe how the bowl can specifically benefit me; I am a teacher, so I could use it to focus my students' attention. I could also use it as a prop for a fun class exercise. With this, I am far more likely to buy their bowl. Is this because I am selfish and don't care about their need to sell the bowl? No. But I am more willing to say yes when I know that this person is thinking of me, not just themselves.

Now, let's bring these principles back to your fundraising event. You have shared from a genuine, heartfelt place why you're doing it. Next, you will explain to your listeners what's in it for them. You have to know something about your potential sponsors or attendees to be able to highlight what would be of particular interest or benefit. If you're talking to those new to the city, let them know the event will be a great way to meet new people. If you're pitching potential business sponsors, you could point out that it will expose their brands to key industry professionals. This doesn't mean you should exaggerate the benefits; be honest in all your dealings, but try to express the advantages in a way that will resonate with your target audience.

You could meet with a hundred people who like your project, but your efforts will be completely worthless unless you move to the next step: making the invitation. Encourage folks to take concrete action like buying a ticket, volunteering their time, sponsoring a prize, or donating money. Give them options; if someone can't help with one aspect, they may be able to assist you in other ways or connect you to someone who can help. Be clear—not only about what you need, but what they will receive for their contribution. You have little to lose in asking, and they may actually be flattered by the request.

While remaining open-minded, focus on hearing yes and the possibilities that can open up from that word. Saying yes to your project is a chance for others to contribute something to their community—an opportunity for them to learn, grow, feel good, and help others feel good. And when you say yes to their engagement in your project, you are building bridges. Don't forget to say yes to other people's requests for help as well.

What If You Get a No?

While contributing to a greater cause is a benefit in terms of how it makes you feel, you can't assume everyone will want to work for *your* cause. You have shared from the heart, given a good pitch, and made a compelling invitation—but what if these people simply aren't interested? Well, thank them for their time and move on. There's no point in trying to convince them. People don't like to feel pressured, so try not to be too pushy. Not only will this upset them, but it can tarnish your reputation. That's why it's important to give the other person space to say no, and for you to be genuinely okay with that response. It doesn't necessarily mean your offer is unappealing, nor does it mean that you somehow failed in demonstrating the value of your request. There are literally hundreds—perhaps thousands—of reasons why someone might turn you down. Most of them have nothing to do with you. Heed the advice of Michael Redhead Champagne: "Focus on those who show up, not on those who don't."

Besides, getting no on a few occasions is a good sign, indicating that you're making some big, bold requests. Hearing yes is exciting; it can lead to endless possibilities and feels really good. But if you only receive yeses to your requests, this may be a sign you're playing it too safe or not setting your sights high enough. On the flip side, if you don't get any, you might want to reassess your approach and find a better way to express the opportunity you're offering. Of course, no matter how you frame your pitch, the chances of folks making a commitment will be greater if you already have strong connections within your communities, as well as a compelling vision. When you work from a place of values and passion, you will attract people of similar values and passion. The heart is more powerful than the head.

Our social connections can be thought of in a number of ways—like threads in a strong web, bridges spanning communities, or even those interwoven tree roots in the forest. The important thing to remember is this: the strength of all these systems relies on healthy, nourished connections. Our hearts and dreams may be boundless, but in practical terms, we only have so much time and energy. So, quality definitely outweighs quantity when it comes to ties with others. The deeper we connect, the more power we have collectively to make a difference to each other and the world. To quote the American anthropologist Margaret Mead, "Never doubt that a small group of thoughtful, committed citizens can change the world. Indeed, it is the only thing that ever has."

Week 6 Lesson Summary

- Long before you ask others to get involved in your projects, start working regularly on broadening and deepening your relationship ties, both weak and strong.

- Strengthening your connections is good for everyone, including you.

- Ask yourself what you can do for others, then do it—without expecting anything in return.

- If you want to make an idea come alive, first get connected with the *why* of your vision and how that makes you feel. Use the power of emotion to connect to others before giving them practical reasons for supporting your venture.

- Think about how your endeavor can be an opportunity for others. Let them know how their participation can benefit them: socially, business-wise, emotionally, etc. Present a clear invitation to get involved.

- Focus on the possibilities of *yes*. But be gracious and give people the space to say no. Remember that getting a few rejections is a good thing. It means you're stretching yourself and making some bold offers.

Week 6 Exercises

1. YOUR COMMUNITY TIES

Take a piece of paper and create two vertical columns. Label the first column "Strong Ties" and the second column "Weak Ties." Now, brainstorm at least ten names in each column. Try to include a range of people from different communities that you belong to (family, work, school, social networks, religious groups, your neighborhood, etc.).

2. HELL YES!

Think about how you can be of service. When you say yes to others, you are strengthening ties and creating new opportunities. In addition, the people you help may one day say yes to your own request. So, if you're ready, challenge yourself this week to *be* a yes. This may mean a shift in attitude, but see how it makes you feel afterward. Don't overextend yourself, but be aware of all the possibilities.

3. MEDICINE WHEEL

Choose a project that's in the early idea/planning stages—one that requires you to engage with others in your community. I suggest you continue to work on the five-year project you sketched out last week, although you don't have to. Feel free to dream up something else, even just for the purposes of this exercise.

Draw a big circle and divide it into four by drawing an X through it. This is your Medicine Wheel. Label the four quadrants: Spirit, Body, Heart, and Mind. In each space, jot down some thoughts and ideas related to engaging people at each stage of your project.

Spirit: What's your vision for the project? What purpose does it serve? How does it better the world? Who are some of your "safe" people, who can be trusted to provide support, feedback, and ideas at this early stage of the process?

Body: What are the goals and expected benefits of your project? How do you see getting started—and staying on track? Who could provide assistance, constructive feedback, or resources?

Heart: Why are you pursuing this dream? Take some time to center yourself and connect with your emotions around the project. What are some words and images that come up for you? Your emotions are an important tool. They are not only part of what helped create this idea, but also a powerful way to convey the salience and potency of your idea to others. Can you think of a succinct story that helps to get across your project's emotional dimensions?

Mind: Are there any concrete examples that illustrate the value of your project? What statistics or research results could you use to communicate its credibility? What value does it provide to the people you'd like to see involved in this project? What's in it for them?

4. GET RESOURCEFUL

Make a list of all the resources you will need to achieve your project goals (skills, information, materials, money, etc.). Be as specific as possible.

For each resource that you need, brainstorm a list of people who could assist you with obtaining it. Consider both strong and weak ties, and remember that support can mean labor, funding, mentoring, in-kind donations, marketing help—there are so many possibilities. Now, select one person from that list and write a pitch asking them to take part in your project. Make this a few concise sentences. Be clear about how this person's involvement will be of benefit. How can you express this in a brief yet authentic, compelling way?

Next, write a direct invitation requesting the kind of help that you have identified. Again, keep it short and be clear about what you're asking them to do.

Now that you've done this thought experiment, ask a friend to role-play a conversation between you and the potential helper. Ask your friend for feedback, then try different ways of making your pitch and invitation and see how they land.

Weekly Challenge: Get Connected

This week's challenge is to do one thing a day to strengthen your community ties.

Take a look at your list of strong and weak ties and choose seven people. Make sure that your selection includes names from both categories.

For each person, come up with an action you can take to strengthen that tie.

For strong ties, your activities might include sending a thank-you card to a friend, making a conscious effort to talk with your neighbor, or asking your coworker about their life.

For weak ties, you may want to consider reaching out to someone you haven't talked to in a while, hosting a dinner for people you would like to know better, or asking someone you've just met to grab a coffee with you.

These acts don't need to be monumental or time-consuming. Simple gestures done regularly can also add up to a big impact—to you, and to your communities. Getting connected means getting happier and healthier, and is one big step closer to realizing your vision.

Don't forget to journal about your experiences with this weekly challenge before moving on to Week 7. For more direction, refer to the guide for self-reflection in the Appendix.

WEEK 7

OBSTACLES: BLASTING THROUGH ROADBLOCKS

It's the action, not the fruit of the action, that's important.
– MAHATMA GANDHI

Marion Ravenwood: Where are you going?

Indiana Jones: Through that wall.*

IMAGINE A GOAL. ONE THAT WOULD BE A STRETCH FOR YOU. Perhaps you want to start a business, create a public art project, or organize a fundraiser for a good cause. You've got it all mapped out. Your vision is clear, your ask is compelling, and you have built a solid plan. Now people are jazzed and want to get involved. So, you get to work. Step-by-step, you complete each task set out in your plan. Everything goes exactly as expected and you successfully complete your project with ample time to spare. The crowd goes wild!

**Raiders of the Lost Ark* (1981)

But there's a problem. This is a fairy tale: a tall tale that has about as much to do with reality as an Indiana Jones film. Things never go as smoothly as planned. There will always be unexpected challenges that will take you off course. That's just part of life.

In practice, your path toward a goal will probably look something like this. You start off with a surge of energy and make some immediate gains. Before long, you encounter a roadblock that stops your progress. You spin your wheels for a short time, deal with it, and keep moving forward. Suddenly, a major crisis hits, which knocks you off course. You must quickly manage the crisis to get back on track. With your deadline looming, you make a final mad dash to the finish line. Forced to pull an all-nighter, you just barely complete the goal without a moment to spare. It wasn't pretty and it was far from perfect, but you got there in the end.

As we saw in Week 5, goal setting is a powerful practice for translating your vision into smaller, doable chunks involving concrete tasks and clear deadlines. However, even if your goals seem foolproof, there's no guarantee you'll achieve them. But I *can* guarantee that this journey will require plenty of hard work, determination, and acceptance.

You can map out the way, but there will be detours. Roadblocks can be costly to ignore—financially, energetically, and psychologically—so you might as well deal with them head-on! This week, we'll explore how to blast through roadblocks standing between you and your final destination.

Get Out in Front

The first step to overcoming your obstacles is to realize that they exist. Once you accept that, you will be better able to anticipate some of them. By identifying the roadblocks you are likely to face, you will be prepared to address them if and when they pop up. It's not possible, or even realistic, to assume you will be able to predict and prepare for every contingency, but a little advance preparation in this area can greatly improve your chances of success.

A note about obstacles versus limitations. Broadly speaking, obstacles are differentiated between those you have no control over and those you can influence. An obstacle that cannot be changed or removed is a true limitation, like time; we only have a certain number of minutes in a day, days in a year, and so on. You cannot magically produce even one more second of time, and unless someone invents time travel, you're out of luck. So, when it comes to limitations, there is no point worrying about what you cannot change. Accept real limitations and plan accordingly, but don't waste your valuable energy trying to change them.

In contrast, what seems like a limitation is sometimes just an obstacle that can be removed, worked around, or transformed in some way. For example, although we can't control time, we can work on our time management skills by learning to delegate and prioritize more effectively. We might also face personal barriers like a lack of education or a tendency to procrastinate (I am guilty of this one). Or we may encounter external barriers, like the cost of obtaining information, or a lack of connections. All of these obstacles can be overcome once identified. There are two ways to approach obstacles. The first is to come up with solutions on the fly. Sometimes this is unavoidable, but the second approach is better: get out in front and anticipate obstacles before they're in your face. This takes foresight and discipline, but it's an investment that will save energy, time, and (probably) money along the way.

A good way to spot potential obstacles *and* solutions is to revisit the goals you have mapped out for your project. Only this time, when you consider all the tasks involved in accomplishing your goals, let yourself imagine all the possible roadblocks. Be brutally honest and try not to gloss over anything. Ask yourself if you lack any of the specific skills required or if there are connections with people or organizations that need to be made. Look at your financial resources and compare them to what you'll need. And don't forget to tap into your emotional state. Are you afraid of getting started or of failing? Do you lack confidence in your abilities? Write everything down.

Next, try to separate the obstacles you have the power to control from the ones you do not. Let go of the latter group. With the ones you can influence, brainstorm solutions for each. Feeling stuck? Call for reinforcements by getting an outside eye. Asking other people for input, especially if they're skilled problem-solvers, creative thinkers, or have experience on similar projects, can provide fresh perspective and insight. They can help you uncover unforeseen hurdles and—just as valuable—solutions you may not have considered. You'll have a chance to try this for yourself in the exercises at the end of this week's chapter.

Obstacle to Opportunity

Okay, you've put in the work of identifying possible roadblocks on the path ahead. But what about addressing the way you perceive challenges that come your way? The first step is taking responsibility for your obstacles and recognizing that you have the power to overcome many roadblocks that you will face. In fact, you can take it even further by learning how to view obstacles as opportunities. This is not necessarily easy or clear-cut, but there are ways to mentally prepare for inevitable setbacks (and occasional failures). You can learn to develop the right mindset to transform even the toughest challenges.

Let's say you're about to launch a small social enterprise with a mission to improve the lives of people in a disadvantaged community. You have a fantastic product, but you require a sales and marketing strategy. If you don't have the requisite skills to carry out this task, then you're facing a personal obstacle.

You could view the obstacle negatively, or you could adopt a more positive outlook and ask yourself the question, "What is the opportunity here?"

Seen this way, there is a clear opportunity to learn. In an ideal world, we would all be continually sharpening our tools and expanding our repertoire with a practice of lifelong learning, but let's be honest: we don't always have the time, energy, or motivation to do this. So, a roadblock can serve as a powerful incentive to improve ourselves. Given the availability of information, resources, tools, and training options online, it's easier than ever to acquire practical skills at a low cost, and many of these things are transferable to other projects. An investment in your own learning can ramp up your impact on the world.

Maybe you don't have the capacity (or inclination) to boost your own learning. No problem! This could be an opportunity for partnership, either with another individual or an organization. Notice that I use the word "partner" instead of "hire"; it's an important distinction. A partnership implies a mutually beneficial arrangement, not a one-way, pay-for-service transaction. The key to a successful partnership is to think win-win. This requires a shift in perspective, with the objective of maximizing the benefits for both of you. Basically, you are working from the "What's in it for them?" principle that you practiced last week.

You know why you want to partner with *them*, but why would *they* want to partner with *you*? If you are dealing with individuals, consider whether working together would also serve their goals and values. This is a highly motivating factor for most people. Next, look at their skills. Do they have the right tools to help you? What tools do you have that might help them? And how can you help clear the way to achieving their goals? There are multiple ways that being in partnership with you could be beneficial; it is your job to make that benefit clear. By thinking in terms of opportunities for them, you might just discover new opportunities for yourself, too.

When approaching a business for a potential partnership, consider motivators like money, reputation, and reach. Many businesses have funds earmarked for charitable giving that they must distribute every year, including "in kind" gifts. They will want their giving to be aligned with their corporate values—something they are proud to promote, which enhances their reputation with their customer demographic. It just takes a bit of research and awareness of their needs.

Whether wooing a person or a business, never make the mistake of expecting virtue to be its own reward. Give them the ol' Gandhiana Jones treatment—throw some fun and benefit for them in there as well.

When I launched my Better World Tour, I wanted to promote it widely. With this in mind, I reached out to one of the biggest newspapers in the country with a partnership request. In exchange for ongoing promotion of the project, we offered to provide the paper with content, photos, and stories, plus the goodwill benefits of being a key partner of an upbeat and inclusive cross-country campaign. Newspapers get inundated with requests for promotional support, so I framed my pitch as a mutually beneficial opportunity. The newspaper saw the value in my proposal, and that helped to secure the deal.

It's satisfying to strike up a partnership where one naturally exists, but it can be a cumbersome and inefficient process when you just need something done well and quickly. Sometimes, hiring the skills and services you need can serve you better than partnering. But a lack of financial resources can be an obstacle in itself. No fear—there could still be opportunities, if you're willing to get creative. For example, the other party might be open to a commission-based or profit-sharing arrangement, which can reduce your financial risk if the project stumbles while increasing gains for them if it does well. Don't assume that cash is the perk of choice. It's a predictable one, but many of us jump at the invitation to participate in something novel and meaningful as a reward in itself. The chance to exercise skills and creativity outside our normal routines—with little risk and potential recognition—can be highly motivating. Working with you may allow someone to add to their portfolio or CV, or broaden their network, which can lead to even more opportunities.

If you only act in your own self-interest, it can be challenging to get outside help at a price you can afford. Although it is sometimes necessary to pay top dollar, the reality is that you'll be able to accomplish more with less if you can think in terms of win-win. You'll usually have an easier time if you take a more cooperative approach and work with partners to ensure that everyone benefits. This is a proactive and creative approach, which views obstacles as genuine opportunities for you and others. The good news is that even if this style of thinking doesn't come naturally to you, there are ways to cultivate it, which we'll explore next.

Optimizing Optimism

Through the years, my mom has given me the same response whenever I've faced trying times: "Things always have a way of working out for you, Joe."

For a long time, although I appreciated the sentiment, I admittedly chalked it up as a motherly platitude and was not sure I could extract any sage advice from her words. I could feel the affection and care but still couldn't see how to improve a bad situation. I'm all for being optimistic, but to think that a positive outcome is somehow preordained strikes me as Pollyanna thinking: too passive and idealistic to be realistic.

Then a surprising thing happened. I was facing a professional setback when, suddenly, my mom's message popped out of the recesses of my mind and lodged itself right in my frontal lobe. "Things always have a way of working out for you, Joe." Only this time, I heard it differently. I realized that this wasn't a passive statement in the least; things would work out for me because I have the ability to make them work out.

Now, anytime I'm knocked down, I pick myself up and focus on how I can overcome the problem at hand. I look for ways to create opportunities. "Things always have a way of working out" has become a call to action and a testament to the transformational power of optimism.

Nurturing a positive mental outlook doesn't mean viewing the world through rose-colored glasses; it is about cultivating a proactive and open-minded attitude to resolving problems. With a positive mindset, you will be better equipped to deal with life's challenges in a constructive way. You will also be more likely to view obstacles as momentary setbacks on your path to success and take actions to create positive change, rather than fixating on things outside of your control.

The field of positive psychology investigates the aspects of human experience that create happiness and well-being. Barbara Frederickson, a psychology professor at the University of North Carolina, has made this her specialty, and her book *Positivity* explains her "broaden and build" theory of positive emotions. It proposes that negative emotions keep us focused on problems, which is a survival-based way of thinking. In contrast, positive emotions broaden our minds and expand our range of vision, making us more receptive and more creative. In this way, positive emotions help build psychological resilience over time, allowing us to discover and build new skills, knowledge, and connections, which we can draw upon when an obstacle (or opportunity) presents itself. Viewed from an evolutionary perspective, Fredrickson argues that positive emotions have a grand purpose in human progress and underlie many of our extraordinary achievements in culture, art, medicine, and technology.

People who experience more positivity tend to interpret obstacles as transient, controllable, and specific to one situation. Humans are more creative, constructive, open, and receptive to new ideas when we're in a good mood, which helps us to innovate and find new and better solutions to the obstacles we face. And, if an unsurmountable obstacle should present itself, those with a positive mindset are more sanguine about failure and optimistic about the future.

This is good news for those of us who naturally have sunny dispositions, but what about folks with a more cynical outlook on life? It turns out that anyone can cultivate a positive mindset by making small, regular changes in their routine. Examples include spending time with positive people, going for walks and exercising, reading inspiring stories and quotes, listening to uplifting music, keeping a gratitude journal, meditating, and visiting places that make you happy. Another piece of good news is that you really can "fake it 'til you make it," as going through the motions of something can actually change your feelings around it.

The payoff from nurturing a positive mindset is significant. It can help to improve job performance, increase your chances of financial success, improve self-confidence, boost energy levels, and promote overall well-being.

Positivity can even help you live longer, as one landmark study proved. Researchers wanted to examine the degree to which a positive or negative approach to life affects health and longevity. They decided to focus their study on a group of nuns who cohabitated, sharing similar diets, daily routines, and other living and working conditions: an ideal situation for controlling the factors that would influence the study.

Drawing from data that spanned sixty years, the researchers found that the nuns who expressed more positive emotions lived a decade longer on average, had lower mortality rates, and were less impacted by serious disease (particularly Alzheimer's) than their counterparts who expressed more negative emotions.

Why is this? A number of scientific studies have found that positive emotions boost the immune system, while negative emotions have the opposite effect. People with a positive outlook are also better able to cope with everyday stress and life challenges. Not a bad return on a simple investment in yourself.

Here's another remarkable thing about positivity: much like kindness, it's infectious. Being positive around another person, and sharing affirmative words and helpful actions, has the effect of releasing the hormone oxytocin into the bloodstream. This chemical reaction floods the body with positive feelings of love, joy, and connection.

Learning about the proven power of positivity made me reflect on my mom's advice. Her words have always proven true, but there was an added gift that transcended their literal meaning: the spirit of her positivity took root in me and inspired me to tackle life's challenges. Now that I see that, I strive to be more like her.

"Things have a way of working out." If you remember this, it will change your view of outcomes. If you expect success, then even when you experience moments of failure, you'll know it's not the end of the story, and you'll keep going until you succeed. However, if you expect failure, you'll also reach your expected outcome. As Henry Ford said, "Whether you think you can or think you can't, you're right."

Stay Calm, Mindful, and Nonattached

One summer in college, I worked for a company that hired students to paint houses. Looking back, I'm surprised anyone would entrust their home to an inexperienced crew of young people. But the price was right, and people can be sympathetic to students who are trying to make a buck. In addition to the painting itself, we were expected to drum up new business by knocking on doors. I dreaded this at first, as we were turned down repeatedly, but it offered me a crash course in self-confidence.

The more doors I knocked on, the bigger my sample size became, and I noticed that people's reactions were often wildly different, even though I hardly deviated from my script. Cordial conversation and a polite "No, thank you," at one door could be followed by profanities at the next. (It's a myth that all Canadians are polite. I can still remember one guy cursing at me for interrupting his dinner and continuing to yell as I slunk back to the street.)

It dawned on me that people's reactions were largely outside my control—and that this didn't say anything about me personally. The only thing I could control was myself. I'd enter the conversation with energy, confidence, respect, and friendliness, and deliver my message authentically. Whatever followed, my demeanor didn't need to change or affect who I was inside.

I didn't know it then, but I was aligning myself with an ancient Greek philosophy called Stoicism. Founded in Athens around the third century BCE, the school of thought teaches four cardinal virtues: wisdom, morality, courage, and moderation. The Stoics viewed external circumstances as neither good nor bad in themselves, but as valuable opportunities to apply these virtues. To quote the Stoic philosopher Epictetus, "We cannot choose our external circumstances, but we can always choose how we respond to them."

Self-control and self-awareness are concepts central to Stoicism. By viewing external circumstances in a detached manner and suspending any judgments, good or bad, the Stoics sought to remain centered and in control of their words and behavior. This is similar to what Buddhists believe and is what many others aim to achieve by practicing mindfulness and non-attachment. (More about this in Week 8.)

The Stoics engaged in a mind exercise called *premeditatio malorum*, which is a kind of negative visualization. It's not dissimilar to the practice of taking stock of potential obstacles that may await you down the road. The Stoics believed that, by mentally preparing for the fact that negative outcomes can and do happen and imagining them ahead of time, they were inoculating themselves from the effects of terrible circumstances.

To be clear, this wasn't about cultivating pessimism or fixating on the specter of failure; rather, they proposed that we can prepare for the worst while continuing to cultivate an unflappable, optimistic demeanor—staying the course no matter what's happening outside of our control.

Of course, we all prefer happiness and hope for good outcomes, but if we're overly preoccupied with creating the positive, we can actually bring about the opposite. It's paradoxical that what we strive for most is often what eludes us. When we seek pleasure and avoid pain, we are giving control to our external world. But when we can accept what is actually happening without desiring anything different, we gain control of our own response and thus our inner experience, bringing a measure of freedom. This is non-attachment.

You can put your own twist on Stoicism by viewing obstacles as opportunities to live out your own cardinal values, whatever they are. Practicing non-attachment will help shift your outlook on the roadblocks you encounter in life; they'll no longer seem so high, and the fall won't seem so far. Obstacles are to be expected, of course, but rather than viewing them as problems to avoid, you can view them as exercises to strengthen your muscles of intention and focus. You get to decide how to approach difficult situations: with integrity and alignment with your values. You get to identify potential solutions, rather than panicking about potential outcomes and the reactions of others. And you will get to practice this over and over again. So, let go of perfection and look for ways you can improve. It's growth, not perfection, that makes for an interesting life. When you do reach your goals, that's great. Celebrate. But if you don't, remember that there are more important ways to measure your worth. Our actions indeed speak louder than words and money and are worth more than any external recognition we could ever receive.

Over time and with deliberate practice, you'll find it easier to stay calm, no matter the situation. Instead of reacting to external stimuli or getting mired in anger and frustration, you'll have the awareness and self-discipline to choose responses that are aligned with your best self. Incremental practice gets you conditioned for the rough times, and then, once you do meet a serious obstacle face-to-face, you'll have real stamina, and it will be as if you've worked your way through high-altitude training. Afterward, many challenges will seem like a breeze.

This might sound absurd, but I recommend deliberately seeking out small obstacles and making a game out of trying to overcome them. I've done this many times—letting myself goof up and make mistakes, like trying to get somewhere without a map. (Remember my snowy adventure in Boston?)

You could even deliberately court rejection, like author Jason Comely. A tech entrepreneur and self-proclaimed introvert, he set himself this challenge as a way to get over his crippling fear of rejection by turning it into a reward for his efforts. Without knowing it at the time, Comely had based his game on exposure therapy, a psychotherapy technique for curing phobias and extreme fears by exposing a client to the thing they're most afraid of. He started by going up to a stranger in a parking lot and asked for a ride across town. The man said no, and Jason thanked him anyway. Then he asked to cut into the checkout line at his supermarket, requested a lower interest rate from a credit card provider, and tried for discounts at retailers. As he went along, Jason's fear gradually subsided.

Not everyone will want to (nor should you, necessarily) undertake the exact challenge that Jason set for himself. The point is that we all have fears that can be significant barriers to pursuing our goals. Oftentimes, it's not actually a poor outcome that we fear but the interpretation we give to it ("See, this proves I'm a loser"). Be on guard; these are just stories we tell ourselves, and we are capable of changing those stories. Your thoughts and feelings—and even your achievements and failures—are not *you*. This circles back to the idea of non-attachment.

These principles can also help us to navigate the more significant barriers and limitations we all face, especially those that we don't anticipate—a surprise deadline change, say, or an unexpected expense. Roadblocks like these can be hard, and they require us to decide for ourselves how (or even whether) to address them. No matter what, we can still move forward and make constructive choices that are aligned with our personal values.

Embrace Failure

If your goals are ambitious, you will surely face some tough moments along the way. You may encounter significant setbacks, quite possibly resulting in failure. This is to be expected. Failure is a normal part of the human condition.

Among baseball players who have been inducted into the Hall of Fame, the batting average is a smidge over .300 (getting a hit 30 percent of their times at bat). In other words, the best players in the sport's history "failed" a whopping 70 percent of the time! The late Ty Cobb still holds the highest career batting average: .366 over twenty-four seasons. The best there is failed almost two-thirds of the time.

Consultants may not earn seven-figure salaries, nor perform to packed stadiums, but they do share at least one thing in common with pro ball players: failure is part of the game. As a consultant, I have spent days, sometimes weeks, preparing a proposal for a new project that ultimately got awarded to someone else. As a freelancer, I'm not even paid for my time writing proposals, so the sting of financial failure adds to the psychological blow. But, like those Hall of Fame baseball players, I consider a 30 percent success rate quite good.

Failure bites. We can all relate to the sting of a dropped ball or a sour note, or even a relationship breakup. It's tempting to erase the experience from memory, or worse—to try repairing your bruised ego by making excuses or blaming others. Instead, it's better to take a more constructive approach.

Through failure, you can learn what doesn't work, and what you can do differently the next time. Here's my approach. When one of my consulting proposals is turned down, I write to whoever considered my submission and thank them, offering my best wishes for a successful project. I also ask if we can set up a call to debrief, which accomplishes two things. First, it gives me an opportunity to build rapport and strengthen the relationship with a professional colleague (and possibly a future client). Second, it provides a chance to get feedback on the strengths and limitations of my work and possible areas for improvement. This helps me to see things from the client's perspective and to better understand their needs and wants. Not only have these discussions helped me to improve my work, which makes subsequent proposals more competitive, but they've also led to other immediate job opportunities. You never know what doors may open if your mind is open as well.

Failure means that we didn't get the results we hoped for. Now, if we are viewing life through the principles of non-attachment, this is not a problem. But most of us will experience disappointment, self-criticism, and even anger at times. Instead of dwelling on these things, shift your focus to the process. First, reflect back and see if you can identify where things went sideways. What caused this? What actions did you take, or could you have taken, to prevent it? How can you do it differently next time? If this was a project you worked on with others, get the team together to dissect the failure (this is commonly referred to as a "postmortem"). If this was an independent venture, you can do this self-reflection alone. But if you're stuck, and it's something you really want to learn and grow from, then reach out to your network to get feedback (preferably from those who have achieved success in similar areas). They might be able to help you see the problem from new perspectives and offer innovative solutions.

Failure is nothing to fear. Some of the most celebrated people in history had to overcome major hurdles on their path toward greatness. Albert Einstein failed his college entrance exam. Bill Gates's first company tanked. J.K. Rowling's first book in the Harry Potter series was rejected twelve times before a publisher took a chance on it. Henry Ford's first automobile business went bankrupt in a year. Oprah Winfrey was fired from her first television job as a newscaster. Even the man who portrayed my boyhood idol, Indiana Jones, faced stumbling blocks. After Harrison Ford's first small film role, an executive told him that he'd never succeed in the movie business (I'm so glad that he persevered!). Each of them bounced back, wiser and stronger, to leave their mark on the world. The key is to pick yourself up, learn from your mistakes, refine your strategy, move on, and—come what may—try not to take it personally.

The shock of misfortune can jolt us into action. It can provide an opportunity to reinvent ourselves in response to adversity by inspiring us to create something meaningful amid uncertainty and chaos. It can give us the chance to reflect upon our lives and contemplate our future. It can bring us closer to the people, things, and values that we care about, reminding us what matters most. And it can serve as a catalyst for conceiving new dreams and rediscovering old ones. Ultimately, failure can have many silver linings, as long as we're willing to learn from it.

Week 7 Lesson Summary

- The first step to conquering your obstacles is to identify them so you can plan ahead and take action to overcome them. Make sure to distinguish between obstacles and true limitations.
- If you think of obstacles as opportunities rather than barriers, it can completely shift how you approach them.
- If you cultivate a positive mental outlook on life, you'll be better equipped to deal with obstacles in a constructive, proactive way. You'll be more likely to view failure as a momentary setback on your path to success and then take positive steps to forge ahead, rather than dwelling on things outside of your control.

- We all want the best possible outcomes for our efforts, but it can sometimes be helpful to imagine the worst that can happen. That way, you're mentally prepared for anything. An attitude of nonattachment will allow you to be calmer and more centered, however things go.

- Guess what? You won't succeed at overcoming every obstacle you face. You are going to stumble at some point, and that's normal. If you don't, you may be playing it too safe. Learn to embrace failure as a natural part of growth and a good indicator that you're stretching yourself beyond your comfort zone.

Week 7 Exercises

1. ANTICIPATE ROADBLOCKS

Let's return to the goals you created for your five-year project from Week 5. For each goal, try to come up with a couple of possible roadblocks that you might encounter. Ask yourself if you lack any of the specific skills required, or if there are connections with individuals or organizations that need to be made. Consider your financial needs. Don't forget to include an honest assessment about your own capacity at this present time. Is motivation a challenge? Do you have any fears associated with this project? Write down everything that comes to mind.

2. OBSTACLE OR LIMITATION?

Now, try to separate the obstacles you have the power to control from the ones you do not. If you have no power over it, then it is a limitation. Let go of it. The remaining items are obstacles, and you do have the power to change them. For each obstacle, brainstorm as many solutions as possible. (If you're stuck, you can always seek a fresh perspective and ask trusted friends or collaborators, especially if they are creative thinkers or have had experience in the area you're focusing on.)

3. FROM NEGATIVE TO POSITIVE

Think about a few experiences or events that haven't gone as well as you would have liked, recently or in the distant past, and jot them down. For instance, maybe you had an argument with a friend, burned a meal, or arrived late for an appointment.

Pick one of these experiences, then answer the question: What is one positive thing that came from that event? Perhaps your argument allowed you to see a different perspective on an issue that you would never have imagined. Perhaps your burned meal led you to meet someone new at your local diner. Maybe your late arrival meant you got to spend time seeing cherry blossoms along the boulevard while you were stuck in traffic. Even if you can't think of anything that obvious, there is always something positive to find in any situation. Now, try another one from your list. And maybe another.

4. THINK LIKE A STOIC

Next, try something almost completely opposite and focus on the negative. Jot down a few upcoming events that you are looking forward to. Pick one and write out a scenario where this event goes horribly wrong. Let's say it's your upcoming birthday party. What if you trip and break your nose and wind up in a hospital?

These are not fun things to contemplate, but you can actually have fun with this exercise by making it as dramatic as possible. The more specific, the better.

Next, write a scenario where you respond to this with calmness and a sense of equanimity, in alignment with your best self and not attached to a specific outcome. Get specific and pay attention to how you feel. You may actually find, if you let go of any disappointment, resentment, or fear about negative outcomes, that you circle back around to finding the positive in your *premeditatio malorum*.

Weekly Challenge: Count Your Blessings

This week's challenge is to keep a daily gratitude journal that will help you to nurture a positive mindset. Get ready to immerse yourself in a daily dose of positivity. Here's your task: At the end of each day, write down three things you are thankful for. In addition, make a note of your biggest accomplishment from that day. (I call this your daily "bright spot.")

There are many things in life to be grateful for. They can be simple moments, like watching a sunrise, receiving a card from a friend, or hearing your favorite song on the car radio. Or they can be more fundamental, like good health, enduring friendships, and safe living conditions. My advice is to write down anything that comes to mind, large and small, that adds value to your life.

Keeping a gratitude journal has been proven to help us form positive memories, which in turn can give us impressions to draw on when we need to boost our mood. For example, a few years ago, I saw a bald eagle soaring high above the ocean not far from my home. That evening, I wrote in my journal about how grateful I was for living in an area with such abundant natural beauty. Even though a few years have passed, I can still recall this moment with clarity, as well as the elation and awe that I felt. The eagle was in sight for only a minute, but the positive memory has lasted for years—partly because I expressed my gratitude in writing. Five minutes a day adds up as you cement good memories to enjoy time and again. So, count your blessings!

Don't forget to journal about your experiences with this weekly challenge before moving on to Week 8. For more direction, refer to the guide for self-reflection in the Appendix.

WEEK 8

SELF-CARE: BOOSTING YOUR RESERVES

Above all, do not forget your duty to love yourself.
- MAHATMA GANDHI

Don't worry...this is kid's play.
- INDIANA JONES*

IMAGINE THAT ONE OF YOUR LIFE GOALS IS TO RUN A MARATHON. But here's the catch: You have never even completed a race of three miles, let alone twenty-six. Undeterred, you register for the event months in advance. The weeks pass, but you don't bother to do any training. In fact, you don't even leave the couch. When race day arrives, you put on your untouched running attire and join the other competitors at the start line. Not long into the race, you're forced to drop out due to utter exhaustion. Failure. Of course, this outcome is unsurprising. It would be foolish to attempt a marathon without proper training. What would be surprising is if

Indiana Jones and the Last Crusade (1989)

you somehow managed to finish the race *without* any preparation.

Throughout the book, I've likened this eight-week course to a journey. But sometimes, becoming the change you want to see feels more like a marathon. It's highly rewarding but, frankly, it's also hard work. It takes dedication and commitment to be successful. And as with a marathon, there are things you can do to prepare for the challenge. The key to success is bolstering your inner reserves to help you stay the course over the long run, so that you have maximum vitality to pursue your dreams, overcome obstacles along the way, and contribute.

Sharpen Your Saw

In 1989, Stephen Covey wrote *The 7 Habits of Highly Effective People.* Hugely popular, the book has sold multiple millions of copies in dozens of languages. Weaving together stories and advice from a wide range of successful people, the book presents seven principles, or habits, which offer guidance on effectively accomplishing your goals.

It's a book that everyone should read at least once, and while I won't discuss all seven principles here, I do want to touch on the seventh habit: sharpening the saw. Covey describes it this way: "Sharpening the saw means preserving and enhancing the greatest asset you have: you."

Covey states that, to maintain and increase your effectiveness, you must continually renew yourself in four main areas of health:

- **Body** is your physical constitution. Building reserves in this area means quality exercise, nutrition, and sleep/rest.
- **Mind** is your mental capacity. Strengthen these reserves by reading, writing, pursuing education, and learning new skills.
- **Heart** is your social and emotional well-being. Boost reserves by building strong relationships, performing acts of service, volunteering, helping others, laughing, loving, and sharing.
- **Soul** is your spiritual wellness—that which is beyond the first three categories. Bolster reserves here by meditating, keeping a

journal of reflections, reading contemplative texts, and, if you're so inclined, attending spiritual services or praying.

"Sharpening the saw" means making time to develop each of these core aspects of your life. We all have at least one area that could use some work, but don't attempt to implement a lot of new habits at once or you may find yourself off kilter. It takes time. Start with one or two shifts that will have a big impact. Strive for balance and a lifestyle that gently and consistently reinforces your reserves in all four areas of your health.

We all lead busy lives, and in a world that makes constant demands on our time, carving out some for ourselves is the biggest challenge we face when investing in our own well-being. But quality counts more than quantity. Simple can be powerful. I've found that the most basic activities are the most replenishing, with the bonus that they can renew more than one area of health at the same time. If you can find just a few things that give you maximum rejuvenation, you're more likely to make them a regular part of your life. Here are some of the best ways I've found to reconnect with myself and replenish my inner reserves.

Take a Walk

For centuries, philosophers, artists, and visionaries, from Aristotle to Steve Jobs, have walked to enhance their creativity and well-being. In 1860, if you set foot outdoors past midnight in the City of London, you'd be likely to bump into Charles Dickens on one of his late-night strolls. His famous novel, *Great Expectations*, took shape in his mind on the city's gas-lit streets during the wee hours.

Getting around on foot may be impractical for longer trips, but it's a good option for shorter jaunts around town, especially if you live in a place with safe and well-maintained sidewalks and paths, where a decent selection of shops, restaurants, schools, parks, and other amenities can be found near your home and work.

But why go on foot when you can drive? After all, walking takes longer and can be a nuisance, especially in the rain or when hauling heavy bags or small children. Well, one reason is health. The average driver in North America spends more than fifteen hours a week inside a car. Sitting in a car for two hours a day is stressful and causes long-term health issues. In fact, spending this much time in a vehicle can shorten your life expectancy.

Walking is clearly a healthier option. Experts have found that thirty to sixty minutes per day can reduce the risk of heart attacks, strokes, diabetes, and other health problems. Of course, simply knowing that something is good for you in the long term does not necessarily make you change your behavior in the short term. I'm all for preventing diabetes, but it isn't something I consider before dashing off to the grocery store. The reality is that in the midst of a busy day, the convenience of a car will often trump the long-term health benefits of walking.

If you need to sell yourself on walking, it can be fruitful to think in terms of concrete short-term benefits. Walking is efficient in ways you might not have imagined, and it comes with many perks. I found this out during my yearlong experiment in personal change, when I challenged myself to walk for all trips less than three miles for one month. Conveniently, it turns out that the average human walking speed is about three miles per hour. This made for an easy rule: If my destination was less than an hour away by foot, then I hoofed it. By abstaining from vehicles, I logged an average of four miles a day, which takes approximately eighty minutes. This exceeded what experts consider the daily requirement for a physically active lifestyle (exercise equivalent to walking more than three miles at a moderate pace). So, walking was effectively serving two functions at once: commuting and exercise.

All my walking burned an average of four hundred calories per day. Even though expending the same number of calories running or circuit training would only take thirty or forty minutes a day, walking is obviously less stressful on the body. The adage "No pain, no gain" doesn't really come to mind when heading out for a stroll. Sure, higher-intensity workouts will burn calories in half the time, but they won't get you to the grocery store. In fact, going to the gym may even add to your daily travel requirements. On top of that, you'll likely need to take time to shower and change after your workout. If you factor in the total time out of your day for both transportation and exercise, you may be surprised at how time-effective walking can be.

During my monthlong walking challenge, I not only surpassed my personal daily fitness requirement, I arrived at work feeling (and smelling) fresh, did my shopping on the way home, and was left with free time for other activities. It saved me time, and it also saved me money. When I tallied up everything I would have spent on gas and parking, gym membership fees, fitness clothing, and equipment, I arrived at a significant figure.

Perks aside, let's return to the health benefits. Walking is good for your mental and emotional well-being. It gives you a chance to slow down and clear your head, which can help to reduce stress and boost your mood. By stimulating blood circulation and providing oxygen to the brain, walking also improves cognitive function and gives you more energy. Aside from that, it allows for happenstance and spontaneity; you never know whom you're going to meet or what you might see. It puts you out in the world and makes you open to connections in a way that being stuck in a car does not.

You might not want to go as far as following in my footsteps by ditching the car completely, but taking a more holistic outlook on time management could cause you to rethink your daily choices about travel and fitness. Although walking takes more time than driving, if you factor in the benefits, you might just find it's more appealing.

You Are What You Eat

A few years ago, I committed to making meaningful changes to my diet that would benefit my mind and body. These changes had to be manageable, as my goal was to adopt them for the long haul. After some research, I found that the Mediterranean diet was what I was after. This didn't mean

eating Greek or Italian food per se, but eating a mix of foods that are tradi-
tionally consumed by people of the Eastern Mediterranean region; their
diet is high in fresh fruits, vegetables, and whole-grain cereals; and low in
red meat, animal fats, refined sugar, and highly processed foods. In many
ways, it flips the typical Western diet on its head.

I like eating this way. It's easy, inexpensive, and not overly restrictive,
as it's not based on abstinence but on moderation—a smart principle for
any diet. More important, though, I like how it makes me feel. In general, when I follow the diet guidelines, I feel alert and clear-headed and
have consistent energy levels throughout the day. It's hard to say whether
the dietary changes are the sole contributor to these results, but I'd like
to think what I eat is largely responsible. My observations are consistent with scientific research, which shows that people who followed the
Mediterranean diet for ten days experienced significant improvements
in vigor, alertness, and contentment. They also recorded faster reaction
times on certain memory tasks, which may indicate that the diet helps
to increase the ability to focus. As a bonus, eating this way provides a
healthy way to manage your weight. Add that to the reported long-term
health benefits—including reduced risk of heart disease, cancer, and
even Alzheimer's—and I'm sold on it.

While this diet has been proven to be effective (and works for me),
there are plenty of other dietary approaches that might be better for you.
The important thing is to be conscious about your eating. Most of us put
some thought into what we eat in terms of preferences, but we often don't
put much thought into *why* and *how* we eat. Food is fuel for the whole
human organism. It keeps us alive and keeps our brain, heart, nerves,
and muscles functioning optimally. The nutrients we ingest are micro-
scopic yet mighty, and they become a part of us, so it really does matter
what we eat.

To eat intentionally is to practice self-care. So, pay attention to what
you're putting in your body and how it makes you feel and function. Notice
when, and how much, you're eating. This can make a huge difference.
It's also good to think about where your food comes from, and whether

that aligns with your values. Many people are turning to plant-based diets, while others extol the benefits of a raw diet. Regardless of what you choose, there is no question that consuming fresh, home-prepared food is healthier than processed food and eating out. So, if you have the time and energy, find a new recipe or dig up an old family favorite and embrace home cooking. Your nourishment deserves your loving care and attention. Ultimately, you want to find a healthy approach to eating that works for you: one that's easy to follow, fits your lifestyle and budget, and will keep your reserves topped up for your life's journey.

What we drink is perhaps even more important than our food. Up to 60 percent of the human body is water, so don't forget your eight glasses a day. Dehydration is a major contributor to many illnesses. Depending on where you live, you might want to consider having a water filter in your home to ensure that what you consume is as low in chlorine, heavy metals, and particulates as possible. Keep it clean.

Pull the Plug

What's your biggest vice? While I am quick to defend pleasure, most of us have at least one guilty pleasure that's become a bad habit. Common vices like drinking, smoking, and eating too much junk food have a negative impact on both individuals and society. Few would argue with this. But what if we added the use of personal technology to that list of unhealthy vices?

One 2017 study found that US adults spent almost ten hours a day on average consuming media through televisions, computers, mobile phones, and other connected devices—and these are pre-COVID numbers. Sure, all of our technology is incredibly useful, and some of it essential, but it comes with negative effects that are calculable.

Staring at a screen for nearly ten hours a day can cause eyestrain, headaches, and vertigo. Sitting for long periods contributes to back pain, muscle tension, indigestion, and poor circulation, and it increases the risk of obesity and heart disease. There's also evidence that exercise can't fully compensate for the damaging effects of all that screen time.

Our mental health can suffer too. Social media junkies often show symptoms of depression, disengagement, poor social skills, and a lower ability to empathize (fittingly coined "Facebook Depression"). Children are especially prone to this. The risk of psychological difficulties is much greater for children who log more screen time than their counterparts.

Almost all of our interactions with technology include advertisements, and most of us are exposed to at least one hour of ads every day. Advertising is by definition designed to influence our choices, and studies show that we are being swayed toward overconsumption.

So, how about unplugging? I'm not suggesting an abrupt and complete disconnection, but even just taking a break is worth trying. Ignoring our handy devices means sacrificing convenience when contacting friends, finding our way somewhere, getting information, or locating service providers. To avoid making life unnecessarily difficult, you can plan ahead.

Author and lifestyle guru Tim Ferriss advocates scheduling a twenty-four-hour break from technology every weekend (so as not to interfere with workweek commitments). Confirm your social plans on Friday night before going offline. Remember, those of us over a certain age used to routinely make plans and show up at appointments on time without having to check in online constantly.

Many of us communicate with our friends through one or two lines of text, up to hundreds of times a day. This time adds up, but it's short on real content. Are all those texts and memes really as important or funny as they seem in the moment? Mostly, they're not. A tech hiatus can improve the quality and depth of our communication. When we have more time and fewer distractions, we can be more receptive to substantial in-person conversations that foster meaningful dialogue, better social etiquette, and deeper empathy.

For those who work on a computer, are on call, or need to be in contact with family, you'll have less flexibility in terms of going offline. As a compromise, I suggest minibreaks. In your downtime, how about reading a book instead of going straight for Netflix? Or putting the phone away a couple hours before bed, instead of tucking yourself in with your device?

Unplugging may slow you down in some ways, which might feel strange at first, but there are numerous benefits. You'll have more time to enjoy the real world: to socialize with friends, be outdoors, play sports, and pursue your favorite pastimes. Maybe you'll even learn a new skill or two.

Over time, the discomfort of reduced technology usage will decrease, and your well-being will increase. For those who dare to try something more substantial, read on! But before starting a serious technology cleanse, be advised that the psychological and physical withdrawal symptoms of abstaining from personal devices can be comparable to those experienced by drug addicts or smokers trying to quit. Experts call this Information Deprivation Disorder; and its symptoms include panic, feelings of isolation, and mood swings. Rather than risk sudden withdrawal by dropping these devices cold turkey, a wiser course of action would be to gradually build up toward a complete technology hiatus. Here's my four-week plan:

- **Week 1** starts with switching off the television. This includes live and on-demand TV. Despite the rising use of laptops, tablets, and smartphones, traditional television still accounts for a large part of our total screen time. Tackle the elephant in the room first.

- **Week 2** adds internet surfing to the list of banned activities. Say goodbye to Facebook, Twitter, YouTube, and other non-work-related websites for the rest of the month.

- **Week 3** extends to personal email and instant messaging. Tip: Set up auto-reply messages to explain your whereabouts and request that people contact you by phone if necessary.

- **Week 4** invites you to cut back on cell phone use. Only use your phone for essential calls and texts this week (which means no apps allowed—even maps). This will be enough of a challenge for most of you, but for anyone who wants to take it up a notch...

- **Bonus:** If you're willing and able, give up your cell phone completely and go on a full tech hiatus this week! Refrain from TV, computers, tablets, and mobile phones—all screens off.

If this sounds too difficult, you can try condensing this plan into one week. The withdrawal may feel more severe, but having the end so close in sight should help you hang in there.

From my experience, the toughest part of doing a technology cleanse is being separate from your mobile phone. They're so ubiquitous that they've practically become a physical extension of our bodies, and as such, their sudden absence can be a shock to the system. On my first day of a technology cleanse, I can often feel the presence of my cell phone in my pocket and find myself unconsciously reaching for it.

This got me thinking about how people who've had amputations often report experiencing phantom sensations that their missing limbs are still attached to their bodies. As it turns out, I'm not the first to draw a parallel between the experience of a "phantom limb" and the feeling of being separated from your cell phone; the term "phantom vibration syndrome" has been coined to describe the sensation of feeling your phone vibrate or ring, even when it's not on your person. This is caused by a longstanding dependence on cell phones, and it can be cured by not using your device for a week or two. I've found that the sensation fades rapidly and is typically gone in a few days.

In the days leading up to my first technology cleanse, I braced myself for bouts of loneliness caused by being disconnected from friends. However, I actually felt more connected—to myself. It was like going on vacation without leaving home; time seemed to slow down, I was more open to chance encounters and small adventures, and my senses were more attuned to my surroundings. It was liberating. So, the next time you need to get away from it all, consider loosening the vice grip of personal technologies. It can work wonders.

Meditate to Feel Great

The William E. Donaldson Correction Facility is a maximum-security prison located in Bessemer, Alabama. It's a rough and ruthless place, named after a corrections officer who was killed by an inmate. The prison houses offenders serving lengthy sentences—several hundred serving life without parole—and specializes in managing behaviorally difficult inmates.

Despite its hard-knocks reputation, in 2002, the Donaldson facility established a pioneering meditation program for its inmates. Based on Buddhist teachings, the ten-day intensive retreat helps participants to improve their self-awareness, self-confidence, and hopefulness. The program is voluntary, but it's far from a walk in the park. Participants meditate in complete silence for ten to thirteen hours a day, for ten straight days. Owing to its rigidity, one inmate described the program as "tougher than my eight years on death row."

The benefits are impressive. Inmates who complete the program report lower stress levels, better control of their emotions, improved social skills, and a new sense of peace. This calmness of mind has helped to reduce aggression and other behavioral problems among participants. As evidence, the Alabama Department of Corrections found that inmates who completed the program had a 20 percent reduction in disciplinary action. If meditation can make life better in a maximum-security prison, imagine what it can do for you.

Matthieu Ricard is a Buddhist monk, author, and photographer, originally from France, who now lives in Nepal. After completing his PhD in molecular genetics in Paris in the early 1970s, Ricard decided to forgo a scientific career and instead move to India to study Tibetan Buddhism. In 2008, neuroscientists wired up his skull with 256 sensors as part of a study on hundreds of long-term meditation practitioners. The scans showed that when meditating on compassion (which involves directing kind thoughts and inwardly recited phrases to yourself and others), Ricard's brain registered unusually high levels of activity in the left prefrontal cortex. Elevated activity in this area of the brain is associated with lower anxiety and more positive emotional states. Remarkably, Ricard's levels were the highest ever reported in the scientific literature, and as a result, the popular media dubbed him the "the world's happiest man."

Don't worry—you don't have to move to Nepal and devote your entire life to the practice of meditation to get something out of it. The same study also examined the effects of meditation on the brains of complete novices; the scientists discovered that meditating for only twenty minutes a day for three weeks produces lasting changes in the brain, which help to relieve stress and improve emotional balance.

In my Project Change course, I start each class with a five-minute meditation. As students arrive, what is normally a busy, noisy transition period transforms into a calm, centered beginning to our time together. The first year I tried this, I asked for feedback midway through the semester. One student wrote: "Love it! We rarely take time in our busy lives to sit and breathe. It helps to create focus and a little slice of peace." Another one shared: "Having our classes start with meditation is so refreshing. It helps me to be more mindful in the midst of a full day, and more relaxed and focused in general." I agree. As someone who experiences mild anxiety from time to time, I find that meditating helps to calm my nerves and still my mind. I feel more composed in the classroom, which boosts my teaching performance. Just like going to the gym can improve your physical fitness levels, practicing meditation regularly can positively affect your brain and improve your emotional state. That's good news for you *and* the people you interact with.

We live in a busy world, and this is reflected in our busy minds. Our heads are full of thoughts that are often unproductive, unkind, and not indicative of what's actually going on around us. We could all use a good mental sweep-out. So, it can be very useful to learn some techniques to refocus our attention on the present moment and give ourselves a break from our own thoughts.

There are many different types of meditation, but I would suggest starting with something simple, like the practice I describe in the exercise section of this chapter. It will help you to feel relaxed, but that's not all;

when you learn to become aware of yourself and your surroundings without needing to explain or interpret what you witness, then you are not being controlled by your environment. You are free.

Load Up on Super Activities

Sometimes, taking care of ourselves takes a back seat to other priorities. You know that self-care is important, but how can you squeeze it into your overcrowded schedule?

One way to deal with time constraints is to do activities that provide multiple benefits at once. Eating a healthy dinner with family or going for a bike ride with friends, for example, are good for both your physical and emotional health. Journaling and reading contemplative literature can enhance your mental and spiritual health. These activities are like multivitamins—a single dosage provides more than one benefit to your overall health.

There are even some activities that are so good for you, they boost your reserves in all four areas simultaneously. I call these "super activities" because of the incredible health benefits they provide. You've probably heard of *superfoods*, the term dietitians use for foods like blueberries or kale, which are so packed with nutrients that they're like magic bullets for your body—a one-punch dose of vitamins, minerals, antioxidants, and disease-fighting, immune-boosting compounds. Super activities function in a similar manner: one simple action that can fill your health reserves in the four areas of body, mind, heart, and soul. One of the best super activities of all is free and available to everyone: spending time in nature.

The Japanese have a wonderful expression for spending time in the woods: *shinrin-yoku*, or forest bathing. Its advocates claim that the volatile organic compounds exuded by trees (phytoncides) promote relaxation and reduce stress when breathed in. It's aromatherapy set in the great outdoors.

Whether or not you buy into the aromatherapeutic effects of trees, the general health benefits of being in nature are well founded. Fresh air and natural light are both proven to elevate the mood, while the physical activity of walking or hiking improves brain function, reduces stress, and increases energy levels. In fact, being outside for just twenty minutes a day is enough to boost your vitality. It also increases resilience to illness, promotes longevity, and decreases the risks of mental illness.

The sights and sounds of nature help to reduce our mental fatigue by restoring the brain's power of attention. When mental fatigue is relieved, people are better equipped to manage their problems calmly and thoughtfully, rather than with anger and aggression.

After returning from a hike one day, I sat down to my work refreshed and clear-headed, and I enjoyed a bout of extreme productivity. It felt great—right up until my computer glitched. I lost four hours of work. My regular reaction would have been to slam my desk and shower my computer with expletives. But in this instance, I was surprised by how calmly I responded. I simply took a breath, then got busy recreating all my lost work over the next couple hours. I was certain that my earlier outdoor excursion was a significant factor influencing my response.

It might not surprise you to learn that spending time in nature is good for your mind and body, but have you ever considered how it can help to promote the health of your heart and soul?

Free of the city's distractions and background noise, nature provides a serene venue to connect with ourselves and others. Whenever friends or colleagues join me on excursions outdoors, our conversations seem more genuine, thoughtful, and inspiring than if had they occurred in a busy downtown café. Even strangers seem more willing to exchange pleasantries in natural settings than in urban ones. Research has shown that exposure to nature can shift a person's values and priorities from personal gain to a broader focus on community and connection with others. In short, contact with nature makes us less self-centered and more concerned with the greater good. Nature brings out *our* better nature.

Imagine if every one of us spent some time in nature each day. It's not a stretch to say that we'd live in a healthier, better connected, and more empathetic society. We'd likely treat each other, and the natural environment, with a great deal more respect than we do currently. Knowing that you are helping yourself and the world around you, all while enjoying the scenic beauty of nature, provides an extra incentive to get outdoors more often.

Week 8 Lesson Summary

- Life is busy, and demands on our time are constant; carving out some for ourselves can be difficult, but remember, it's quality that counts more than quantity. Even a few minutes a day can make a big difference. Strive for balance, and regularly do things that replenish your reserves in all areas of health—body, mind, heart, and soul.

- Walking is an easy way to boost your mental and physical health—as well as your social well-being, if friends join in. For shorter trips, challenge yourself to ditch the car and walk instead. It's good for your wallet, too.

- Food is fuel for the whole human organism. Find a healthy approach to eating that works for you: one that's easy to follow, fits your lifestyle and budget, and keeps your reserves topped up. And don't forget your eight glasses of water a day.

- Revel in the rewards of the simple life and go on a technology cleanse. Try abstaining from personal technologies for one day per week, or month. You can gradually build up toward a longer tech hiatus.

- Start your day with a short meditation. Meditating on a regular basis helps to calm the mind and nourish the soul. If you're a beginner or need some extra motivation, you could use a meditation app, watch a guided video on YouTube, or take a class or workshop.

- Spend time in nature. Think of the outdoors as an all-inclusive health club for getting your body, mind, heart, and soul into better shape. Bonus: There are no membership fees.

Week 8 Exercises

1. HEALTHY BALANCE

Here's a quick exercise you can do to assess your current reserve levels. Divide a sheet of paper into four quadrants: Body, Mind, Heart, and Soul. In each quadrant, write down all the things you do regularly to promote good health in these areas. Only list activities you are actively doing at this point in your life. This exercise helps you to identify where your reserves are low. The more balanced you are, the easier it'll be to reach your full potential.

Take note of the quadrant where you have the least activities listed. Brainstorm a few activities that you could try, then pick one and do it this week.

2. PEDESTRIAN POWER

List all your outings from the past seven days. How long were they? What modes of transportation did you use? If you were to plan these trips efficiently, could you substitute walking for some of them? Pick one and try it this week.

Bonus: Challenge yourself to walk exclusively for all trips under three miles. If you can make it to your destination on foot in under an hour, then do it! Of course, adapt the challenge as necessary to reflect your personal abilities.

3. FOOD FOR THOUGHT

Give some thought to what you're putting in your body. Answer the following questions: How does the food you eat make you feel? How does it affect your mood? Your wallet? What are some other implications of your food choices? Are ethical considerations important? Is cooking a passion for you? And are you drinking enough water?

4. TOUGH TECH TALK

Give some thought to the role technology plays in your life, with a focus on reducing your screen time. Read the following questions and answer them honestly: Do you always have your phone with you—during meals, in bed, in the bathroom? Do you spend more than an hour a day watching entertainment online or playing online games? How does this kind of engagement make you feel? What could you be doing in a more active, creative way out in the "real world" that would give you the same feelings?

When you reflect on your answers, is there a place in your life where you could cut down or eliminate your dependence on personal technology? Experiment with that this week.

5. TAKE A MINUTE TO MEDITATE

You can do this easy meditation anywhere, but you might want to begin by putting aside ten to fifteen minutes and finding a quiet room. You can set a timer—ideally something with a soft chime or bell, not a loud alarm. Sit comfortably in a chair or cross-legged on the floor. Close your eyes or focus softly on something in front of you. Notice your breath coming in and going out. Be aware of the thoughts coming to your mind and let them move away. Let your attention drift to any noise coming from outside the room, then refocus on your breath. Continue to notice and let go of anything else that arises, like an itch or other mild discomfort, the urge to get up and check your phone, and so on. Avoid the tendency to explain or judge any thought, sensation, sound, or feeling. When the chime sounds, you're done. That's it—or it's a start, anyway. You can practice extending the amount of time gradually.

6. WHERE THE WILD THINGS ARE

Consult a map to locate all the parks, conservation areas, connector trails, and other natural spaces near your home and work. You may also find useful information about parks and other green spaces by consulting the websites for your city, municipality, or neighborhood.

Weekly Challenge: Go Wild

This week's challenge is to spend thirty minutes in nature every day.

In the most basic sense, nature is any outdoor setting that is untouched and uninfluenced by civilization. Strictly speaking, a park with a maintained trail system and other amenities is not truly in a natural state; however, for most people, spending time every day in authentically wild places is impractical. For the purpose of this challenge, just go somewhere you can see trees and breathe fresh air! If all you can find that fits this description is your neighbor's garden or your local playing field, then you're off to a good start—but strive to go deeper. The more immersed you can be, the better the effect.

Before you start, make sure you have the right gear. You don't want to be half an hour out of the door and realize you're wearing that pair of shoes that pinches your toes. And don't forget to dress for the weather. Optionally, pick up an inexpensive pedometer or download a fitness app to track how far you walk and how many calories you burn. It's a good way to measure the physical benefits of your time outdoors.

Spending time in nature is a perfect way to engage with others. For at least some of your outings, be sure to invite your friends or family to join you. But there will also be times when going solo is what you need to clear your head. Let the serenity of nature uplift your spirits.

Schedule your outings for different periods in the day. A brisk morning walk through a nearby park can provide an immediate boost of energy that carries you for hours. Lunch under a tree can refresh you for the afternoon. Going for a leisurely stroll in the evening can help you to unwind and relax after a hectic day at work.

Don't worry if you're not the outdoorsy type; no one is demanding you go on multiday survival expeditions. Even a simple walk through a wooded park, or a picnic on the banks of a river, can suffice. By spending time in nature in whichever way you find comfortable, you'll not only boost your own inner reserves, but also bring that uplifting energy to the world around you. That's a good reason to go play outside.

As always, don't forget to journal about your experiences with this weekly challenge. For more direction, refer to the guide for self-reflection in the Appendix. Hopefully, you've found journaling to be beneficial to your learning and development over these past eight weeks; if so, consider making it a regular practice as you continue on your journey.

CONCLUSION

In a gentle way, you can shake the world.
- MAHATMA GANDHI

Fortune and glory, kid. Fortune and glory.
- INDIANA JONES*

THERE'S A COMMON MISCONCEPTION THAT PEOPLE WHO CHANGE the world are different from ordinary folks—that they're destined for greatness. That they're special. Not true. Everyone can make change, the effects of which can add up and ripple outward. This takes the courage to dream big, the guts to put this dream into action, and the willingness to have fun along the way.

The four principles are key to becoming a change-maker. Your values are the compass that will guide you on your way. Passion is your fuel. Your skills are the toolkit you'll need as you go. And the footprints you leave behind are the service you give to the world.

Becoming the change you want to see in the world is an aspiration you may find daunting—but it doesn't have to be. This work is not about devoting every aspect of your life to a given cause. That's such a grandiose ambition, it would stop you in your tracks before you even take your first steps. As I've said, it's normal to start small and slow, taking time to experiment and see what fits your goals and personal capacity. With experience,

*Indiana Jones and the Temple of Doom (1984)

you'll get more adept at living in alignment with these principles and integrating them incrementally.

The power of the small is a transformational credo. Even short steps can eventually take you a long way toward bringing yourself more meaning, joy, satisfaction, and connection. This will spill over into other areas of your life and benefit your family, friends, neighbors, community, and the world. In turn, the positive contributions you make to others can inspire them to make a difference in their own circles.

If you give your all every day to whatever you're doing and go to bed satisfied that you've applied the four principles in some way, then one thing will naturally lead to another, and new opportunities will come to you. It's just a matter of time. In addition, practicing self-care daily will build your inner reserves by keeping your body, mind, heart, and soul healthy, which sets you up to be your best self. You'll be making change, whether you can see it yet or not.

Life is meant to be a grand adventure, but we all need to put food on the table, too. Remember, Indiana Jones had a day job—he was an archaeologist! And Gandhi, a powerful agent of global change, also had everyday concerns. But is it possible to be a change-maker, enjoy your life, *and* make a living? Yes, of course it is. The change-makers profiled in this book offer diverse examples of lives based on a congruence of values, passion, skills, and service. They're all leaving positive footprints by impacting their communities and beyond, but they haven't done it alone, and they haven't done it just for others; they're also taking care of their own needs. Being a change-maker doesn't require you to endure a life purely of selfless service. You have to live for yourself as well. Your own livelihood and fulfillment are not only important—they are necessary to sustain you over the long haul.

Gandhiana Jones is a character I made up to symbolize the balance at the heart of a purpose-filled life. Although he might seem like some kind of saint-meets-action-hero, he's actually someone we can all become. Gandhiana Jones serves humanity *and* seizes the day on his epic adventures. And that's the whole point. I'll say it again; too often, a life of service, impact, and change-making is depicted as being in direct conflict with a life of adventure, joy, and pleasure. But it's not a question of martyr versus maverick, philanthropy versus personal gain, or duty versus delight. It's both!

No matter what stage you are at in your life now, you (and you alone) get to choose where to direct your next steps. Your best self is calling you forward, driven by the desire to learn, connect, contribute, and make a difference. The road can be long and sometimes rough, but it is also full of unexpected delights and deeply rewarding relationships. Remember, it's not only the destination that counts, but how you carry yourself each step along the way. There is no time like the present to get out there and *be the change!*

APPENDIX A

ADVICE AND POINTERS

TIPS FOR BRAINSTORMING

///////////////////////////////////////

MANY OF THE EXERCISES PRESENTED IN THIS BOOK ASK YOU TO brainstorm ideas. Here are some recommendations for getting the most out of these exercises. They have worked for me and my students, and hopefully they will work for you, too.

Although it's possible to use a computer or phone to brainstorm, it's far more effective to use a pen and paper. Studies have shown that typing is a more "mindless" task, meaning that the content of what's being typed is not remembered as well as when we write by hand. Writing, printing, and drawing by hand help you to tap into a more creative part of your brain than using a keyboard does. Give yourself a stack of paper or a big whiteboard—maybe some colorful markers—and the freedom to make a mess.

Set a time limit between fifteen minutes and one hour to write or draw anything that comes to mind about the topic, no matter how crazy or tangential it seems. At this early stage, ideas should take precedence over practicalities. Later, you may be able to connect the dots and see a whole new way of approaching your goal or idea.

Remember, there's no right or wrong in brainstorming, so try to avoid the tendency to edit or critique yourself during your session. Easier said than done, right? For me, it's sometimes like having a micromanaging boss looking over my shoulder and suddenly feeling inhibited. You may even hear yourself thinking, *Oh, that idea's stupid.* If this happens and your inner saboteur starts acting up, adopt the role of a facilitator; in group brainstorming sessions, facilitators may politely acknowledge a criticism and then "park it" before quickly moving on. Do the same thing in your own mind. I literally tell my inner critic that it can speak up later, but for now, I need to park my critiques. This keeps me on track and ensures that my ideas keep flowing freely.

If your time is up and you've only generated a few scribbles, that's fine. If you've got pages and pages, even better. But even just one novel idea can help to illuminate your next steps.

GUIDE FOR SELF-REFLECTION

//

THE WEEKLY CHALLENGES IN THIS BOOK ARE DESIGNED TO GET you started. In the spirit of learning by doing, this is a hands-on way for you to access the ideas from the book and apply them in your own life.

To get the most out of these challenges, I encourage you to set aside some time after you complete them to reflect on your experiences. Use a journal for this purpose. It doesn't have to be anything fancy—a simple notebook or a memo on your smartphone will suffice.

Journaling is a powerful tool for personal growth. It provides a structured process to record, interpret, and learn from your experiences. Much more than a diary of your inner thoughts, journaling can help to transform your observations about an experience into deeper awareness and understanding and propel you to create real lasting change in your life.

Instructions: Write an entry in your journal based on each challenge that you complete. What has worked well for me and my students is breaking each entry into four sections using the ORID method (which I've included more information on in the Notes section); ORID stands for Objective, Reflective, Interpretive, and Decisional.

- **Objective:** What are the facts? Briefly discuss what you did for the challenge. Stick to the objective facts in this section.
- **Reflective:** How do you feel about it? Reflect on your gut

feelings about your experience with the challenge. What went well? What did not go as planned? What were the barriers/ obstacles?

- **Interpretive:** What does it mean for you? Discuss the impact that the challenge had on you during the week. What would it mean for you if you stuck with this activity over a longer stretch?
- **Decisional:** What's your next step? The focus in this section is on the future. What changes, if any, will you make based on your experience? What would be the probable outcomes from making these changes?

TWENTY WAYS TO SPREAD KINDNESS

//

1. Help someone with their job search.

2. Put coins in someone else's parking meter.

3. Leave books for neighbors to take from a common area.

4. Take your parent out to lunch.

5. Renew an old friendship by sending a gift to someone.

6. Donate used clothing.

7. Bring your coworkers a special treat.

8. Buy lottery tickets for strangers.

9. Leave a thank-you note for the mail delivery person.

10. Smile at strangers.

11. Buy something for the person in line behind you.

12. Cook a meal for someone.

13. Thank the bus driver.

14. Leave nice comments on social media.

15. Leave a generous tip.

16. Clean up litter on a street in your neighborhood.

17. Hold the door open for someone.

18. Let someone go in line in front of you.

19. Purchase a meal for a homeless person.

20. Give an inspirational book to a friend.

TWENTY WAYS TO STRENGTHEN CONNECTIONS

//

1. Start an online discussion to draw on a group's expertise.

2. Ask someone about their life.

3. Take an interactive class at a community center.

4. Strike up a conversation with a stranger.

5. Acknowledge someone by sending a thank-you card.

6. Patronize locally owned businesses and restaurants.

7. Say hello to people on the street.

8. Attend a community event or festival.

9. Buy food at a farmers' market.

10. Talk with neighbors.

11. Join an online group with shared interests.

12. Host a dinner for people you would like to know better.

13. Connect with older members of the community.

14. Write a letter of encouragement to a local official.

15. Ask others what you can do to help them, then do it.

16. Offer your expertise to someone for free.

17. Give community leaders your input about local issues.

18. Join a Meetup group and attend one of their events.

19. Volunteer for a neighborhood or community project.

20. Reach out to someone you haven't talked to in a while.

APPENDIX B

BIBLIOGRAPHY

RECOMMENDED READING

///

FOR FURTHER READING, THESE ARE THE BOOKS THAT I RECOMmend. This list isn't exhaustive, but it's a good starting point for learning more.

Marcus Aurelius, *Meditations.*

Scott Belsky, *Making Ideas Happen: Overcoming the Obstacles between Vision and Reality.*

Stephen Cope, *The Great Work of Your Life: A Guide for the Journey to Your True Calling.*

Stephen Covey, *The 7 Habits of Highly Effective People: Restoring the Character Ethic.*

Mihaly Csikszentmihalyi, *Flow: The Psychology of Optimal Experience.*

Elizabeth Dunn and Michael Norton, *Happy Money: The Science of Smarter Spending.*

Carol Dweck, *Mindset: The New Psychology of Success.*

Eknath Easwaran, trans., *The Bhagavad Gita.*

Viktor Frankl, *Man's Search for Meaning.*

Barbara Fredrickson, *Positivity.*

Tim Harford, *Adapt: Why Success Always Starts with Failure.*

Chip Heath and Dan Heath, *Switch: How to Change Things When Change Is Hard.*

Ryan Holiday, *The Obstacle is the Way: The Ancient Art of Turning Adversity to Advantage.*

Azim Jamal and Harvey McKinnon, *The Power of Giving: How Giving Back Enriches Us All.*

Robert Maurer, *One Small Step Can Change Your Life: The Kaizen Way.*

Thich Nhat Hanh, *Peace Is Every Step: The Path of Mindfulness in Everyday Life.*

Ken Robinson and Lou Aronica, *The Element: How Finding Your Passion Changes Everything.*

Sharon Salzberg, *The Force of Kindness: Change Your Life with Love and Compassion.*

Martin Seligman, *Learned Optimism: How to Change Your Mind and Your Life.*

Simon Sinek, *Start with Why: How Great Leaders Inspire Everyone to Take Action.*

ENDNOTES

//

Introduction

p. 3, ... *from Mahatma Gandhi.* The actual Gandhi quotation differs from the bumper-sticker version. Here it is, from his writings in 1913: "We but mirror the world. All the tendencies present in the outer world are to be found in the world of our body. If we could change ourselves, the tendencies in the world would also change. As a man changes his own nature, so does the attitude of the world change towards him. This is the divine mystery supreme. A wonderful thing it is and the source of our happiness. We need not wait to see what others do." Mahatma Gandhi, *The Collected Works of Mahatma Gandhi, Volume XII*. New Delhi: Publications Division, Ministry of Information and Broadcasting, Government of India, 1964, p. 158.

How to Use This Book

p. 9, *There are eight challenges...* For one example of how to engage with challenges, watch Matt Cutts's TED Talk, *Try Something New for 30 Days*. In the video, Cutts, a software engineer who worked at Google in the early days, shares this simple but powerful idea: pick something you're curious about or want to add to your life, then do it for thirty days. Some of his challenges involved small tweaks to his lifestyle; he biked to work every day for one month and went without sugar another. Other challenges were huge—dreams that he'd always had but had never acted on. He hiked up Mt. Kilimanjaro, the highest mountain in Africa. He also wrote a fifty-thousand-word novel (requiring him to write 1,667 words a day for a month!). Matt Cutts, "Try Something New for 30 Days," TED2011, March 2011, video, https://www.ted.com/talks/matt_cutts_try_something_new_for_30_days.

p. 9, *There are eight challenges...* Ideally, once you finish this book, you will be looking for new challenges to take on—hopefully, ones that last longer than a

183

week. Seven days is a great start for building a new habit, but depending on what you're trying to achieve, it can take much longer for a new way of thinking and behaving to really take root. A good rule is to stick with a new activity for one to two months to make it habitual. Stretch yourself, if you're feeling bold, to try challenges that last over a longer period. Even a small change in your daily routine can have a substantial impact on your life if you stick with it long enough. For more information on how long it takes for a new habit to form, see: Maria Popova, "How Long It Takes to Form a New Habit: Why Magic Numbers Always Require a Grain of Empirical Salt," *The Marginalian,* https://www.themarginalian.org/2014/01/02/how-long-it-takes-to-form-a-new-habit/.

Week 1: Values: Following Your Compass

p. 15, Marc Stoiber: All material came from an original interview for this book.

p. 19, Julie Phillips: All material came from an original interview for this book.

p. 21, Masa Takei: All material came from an original interview for this book.

p. 24, *All experiences in life are more satisfying...* Elizabeth Dunn and Michael I. Norton, *Happy Money: The Science of Smarter Spending.* New York: Simon & Schuster, 2013.

p. 29, *(If you're struggling to come up with ten values...* For more resources and tips on how to identify your values, see: "What Are Your Values? Deciding What's Most Important in Life", *Mind Tools,* https://www.mindtools.com/pages/article/newTED_85.htm.

Week 2: Passion: Fueling Up for the Journey

p. 32, Melissa Holland: All material came from an original interview for this book.

p. 38, *What does it take?* There are two pertinent books that I've found on the subject of authenticity. *The Five Secrets You Must Discover Before You Die,* by John Izzo, offers precepts for a life worth living. After interviewing over two hundred elders nominated by their friends and families as being pillars of wisdom and joy, the author distilled their collective wisdom into five tenets: "Be true to yourself" is one of them. *The Top Five Regrets of the Dying,* by Bronnie Ware, is a nurse's memoir on the regrets expressed to her by people nearing death. The most common regret of all was: "I wish I'd had the courage to live a life true to myself, not the life others expected of me." What I find particularly interesting is that these two authors come to the same conclusion from opposite perspectives: the former by interviewing older people who have been selected because they have lived rewarding and fulfilling lives; and the latter by speaking with people who are in the last stages of life and are expressing their regrets. The former group of wise elders identify "living true to yourself" as one of the keys to living a fulfilling life, while the most common regret of the latter group is not having the courage to do this very same thing.

p. 40, Holman Wang: All material came from an original interview for this book.

p. 42, *Ride mule, chase horse.* Holman Wang, "'Ride Mule Chase Horse': Down-shifting Your Career the Hard Way," *Possibility of Change,* https://possibility change.com/downshifting/.

Week 3: Skills: Stocking Your Toolkit

p. 47, Matt Carter: All material came from an original interview for this book.

p. 53, *Most high achievers think this way.* Carol S. Dweck, *Mindset: The New Psychology of Success.* New York: Random House, 2006.

p. 56, Kaya Dorey: All material came from an original interview for this book.

p. 57, *... it can feel like a moment of magic.* Mihaly Csikszentmihalyi, *Flow: The Psychology of Optimal Experience.* New York: Harper and Row, 1990.

Week 4: Service: Leaving Footprints

p. 63, Markus Pukonen: All material came from an original interview for this book.

p. 65, Leigh Schumann: All material came from an original interview for this book.

p. 67, Angela Nagy: All material came from an original interview for this book.

p. 68, *... part of the reason they chose their current job.* "Mind the Gaps: The 2015 Deloitte Millennial Survey." Deloitte, 2015.

p. 68, A study featured in the *Journal of Labor Economics* found that happy workers are 12 percent more productive than average. Andrew J. Oswald, Eugenio Proto, and Daniel Sgroi, "Happiness and Productivity," *Journal of Labor Economics* 33, no. 4 (2015): 789–822.

p. 70, ... *improved life satisfaction and well-being, and lower levels of depression.* Caroline E. Jenkinson, Andy P. Dickens, Kerry Jones, Jo Thompson-Coon, Rod S. Taylor, Morwenna Rogers, Clare L. Bambra, Iain Lang, and Suzanne H. Richards, "Is Volunteering a Public Health Intervention? A Systematic Review and Meta-analysis of the Health and Survival of Volunteers," *BMC Public Health* 13, no. 1 (2013).

p. 72 ... *one of the most expensive cities in North America.* Scott Brown, "Vancouver is the 39th Most Expensive City in the World, According to The Economist," *Vancouver Sun*, March 24, 2017, http://vancouversun.com/news/local-news/vancouver-is-the-39th-most-expensive-city-in-the-world-according-to-the-economist.

p. 72, ... *food, transportation, and other expenses.* Social assistance rates in British Columbia: *Government of British Columbia*, s.v. "Income Assistance Rate Table," last updated October 1, 2017, http://www.hsd.gov.bc.ca/mhr/ia.htm.

p. 72, Mark Horoszowski: All material came from an original interview for this book.

p. 75, ... *decided to pick up the tab for the next car.* Elizabeth Fraser, "Random Chain of Kindness at Tim's Goes on for Hours," *Winnipeg Free Press*, January 2, 2013.

p. 75, *Kindness leads to happiness...* Keiko Otake, Satoshi Shimai, Junko Tanaka-Matsumi, Kanako Otsui, and Barbara Fredrickson, "Happy People Become Happier Through Kindness: A Counting Kindnesses Intervention," *Journal of Happiness Studies* 7, no. 3 (2006): 361–375.

p. 75, ... *motivated to be altruistic.* Simone Schnall, Jean Roper, and Daniel M.T. Fessler, "Elevation Leads to Altruistic Behavior," *Psychological Science* 21, no. 3 (2010): 315–320.

p. 76, ... *among other health benefits.* David R. Hamilton, "5 Beneficial Side Effects of Kindness," *HuffPost*, last updated August 2, 2011, http://www.huffingtonpost.com/david-r-hamilton-phd/kindness-benefits_b_869537.html.

p. 76, ... *hidden powers of smiling.* Ron Gutman, "The Hidden Power of Smiling," TED2011, March 2011, video, https://www.ted.com/talks/ron_gutman_the_hidden_power_of_smiling.

p. 76, For more resources and ideas for performing acts of kindness, see the Random Acts of Kindness Foundation's website: https://www.randomactsofkindness.org/.

p. 77, *In a forest, trees share nutrients...*Jane Engelsiepen, "Mother Trees Use Fungal Communication Systems to Preserve Forests," *Ecology Global Network*, October 8, 2012, http://www.ecology.com/2012/10/08/trees-communicate/.

The Four Principles in Harmony

p. 85, *One year, a photo...*Sandra Thomas, "Homeless Tex Donates Trip," *The Vancouver Courier*, November 14, 2004.

Week 5: Vision and Goals: Creating Your Roadmap

p. 90, Meredith Brown: All material came from an original interview for this book.

p. 95, *According to research from the University of Scranton...* Dan Diamond, "Just 8% of People Achieve Their New Year's Resolutions. Here's How They Do It," *Forbes*, January 1, 2013, https://www.forbes.com/sites/dandiamond/2013/01/01/just-8-of-people-achieve-their-new-years-resolutions-heres-how-they-did-it/.

p. 95, *... best ways to make a change in behavior stick.* Chip Heath and Dan Heath, *Switch: How to Change Things When Change Is Hard*. New York: Broadway Books, 2010.

p. 97, *Consider the aptly named S.M.A.R.T. criteria...*George T. Doran, "There's a S.M.A.R.T. Way to Write Management's Goals and Objectives," *Management Review* 70, no. 11 (1981): 35–36.

p. 102, *Reflecting on his cancer diagnosis,...* Steve Jobs's commencement address at Stanford University: *Stanford News*, June 14, 2005, http://news.stanford.edu/2005/06/14/jobs-061505/.

Week 6: Community Connections: Building Bridges

p. 107, Michael Schratter: All material came from an original interview for this book.

p. 111, ... *lower violent crime rates.* Robert J. Sampson, Stephen W. Raudenbush, and Felton Earls, "Neighborhoods and violent crime: A multilevel study of collective efficacy," *Science* 277, no. 5328 (1997): 918–924.

p. 112, Margaret Stacey: All material came from an original interview for this book.

p. 114, *The most significant contributing factor...* Liz Mineo, "Good genes are nice, but joy is better," *The Harvard Gazette*, April 11, 2017, https://news.harvard.edu/gazette/story/2017/04/over-nearly-80-years-harvard-study-has-been-showing-how-to-live-a-healthy-and-happy-life/.

p. 115, *According to Robert Waldinger,...* Robert Waldinger, "What Makes a Good Life? Lessons from the Longest Study on Happiness," TEDxBeaconStreet, November 2015, video, https://www.ted.com/talks/robert_waldinger_what_makes_a_good_life_lessons_from_the_longest_study_on_happiness.

p. 115, For more information on the Harvard Study of Adult Development, see: http://www.adultdevelopmentstudy.org/.

p. 115, Michael Redhead Champagne: All material came from an original interview for this book.

p. 118, *In his TED Talk, Sinek explains...* Simon Sinek, "How Great Leaders Inspire Action," TEDxPuget Sound, September 2009, video, https://www.ted.com/talks/simon_sinek_how_great_leaders_inspire_action.

p. 119, *When teaching my Project Change course,...* The classroom activity in which I challenged students to sell me a meditation bowl is inspired by a scene in the movie *The Wolf of Wall Street*. At the end of the film, stockbroker-turned-business-coach Jordan Belfort (portrayed by Leonardo DiCaprio) asks participants in a sales training seminar to sell him a pen. We share a lot of laughs recreating the scene, which goes a long way in building social capital in the classroom!

Week 7: Obstacles: Blasting Through Roadblocks

p. 133, ... *theory of positive emotions.* Barbara Fredrickson, *Positivity*. New York: Harmony Books, 2019.

p. 134, *Positivity can even help you live longer...* Deborah D. Danner, David A. Snowdon, and Wallace V. Friesen, "Positive Emotions in Early Life and Longevity:

Findings from the Nun Study," *Journal of Personality and Social Psychology* 80, no. 5 (2001): 804–813.

p. 137, *This is similar to what Buddhists believe...* For more information on the practice and science of mindfulness, see: Rick Hanson and Richard Mendius, *Buddha's Brain: The Practical Neuroscience of Happiness, Love and Wisdom.* Oakland, CA: New Harbinger Publications, 2009.

p. 144, *Keeping a gratitude journal...* Robert A. Emmons and Michael E. McCullough, "Counting Blessings Versus Burdens: An Experimental Investigation of Gratitude and Subjective Well-being in Daily Life," *Journal of Personality and Social Psychology* 84, no. 2 (2003): 377–389.

Week 8: Self-Care: Boosting Your Reserves

p. 148, *Experts have found that...* One way to gauge the health benefits of walking is to look at the Amish, who refrain from using automobiles and other modern technologies. According to a 2004 study of physical activity among an Amish community in southern Ontario, Amish men averaged more than 18,000 steps a day while the women averaged more than 14,000 steps per day—well above the 10,000 steps needed to lose weight. It's no wonder that only 4 percent of Amish adults are obese. The Amish lifestyle may not be realistic for most of us, but it does provide a benchmark for daily physical activity. For more information, see: David R. Bassett Jr, Patrick L. Schneider, and Gertrude E. Huntington, "Physical Activity in an Old Order Amish Community," *Medicine & Science in Sports & Exercise* 36, no. 1 (2004): 79–85.

p. 150, ... *typical Western diet on its head.* For more resources and tips on how to follow the Mediterranean diet, see: Colin Tidy, "Mediterranean Diet," *Patient,* June 20, 2016, https://patient.info/health/mediterranean-diet.

p. 150, ... *vigor, alertness, and contentment.* Laura McMillan, Lauren Owen, Marni Kras, and Andrew Scholey, "Behavioural Effects of a 10-day Mediterranean Diet. Results from a Pilot Study Evaluating Mood and Cognitive Performance," *Appetite* 56, no. 1 (2011): 143–147.

p. 151, *One 2017 study...* In 2017, US adults spent almost ten hours a day consuming media via televisions, computers, and mobile phones. Time spent with digital media (including desktop/laptop, nonvoice mobile, and other connected devices) totaled five hours and 53 minutes per day. Additionally, television accounted for three hours and 58 minutes of US adults' average daily time with media. Note that if someone spent an hour watching TV and using a smartphone concurrently, this counted as two hours of total media time. For more information, see: *US Time Spent with Media: eMarketer's Updated Estimates for 2017.* eMarketer, October 2017.

p. 152, *There's also evidence...* Amanda Chan, "Exercise Can't Undo the Damage of Too Much Screen Time," *Live Science,* January 11, 2011, http://www.livescience .com/9257-exercise-undo-damage-screen-time.html.

p. 152, *The risk of psychological difficulties...* Lynne Peeples, "Mental Problems Rise with Kids' Screen Time: Study," *Reuters,* October 11, 2010, http://www .reuters.com/article/us-mental-idUSTRE69A0GD20101011.

p. 153, *... drug addicts or smokers trying to quit.* "Technology Junkies: How We Suffer Withdrawal Symptoms Like Drug Addicts if We're Kept Away from Our Gadgets," *Daily Mail,* last updated January 7, 2011, http://www.dailymail.co.uk /sciencetech/article-1344723/How-suffer-withdrawal-symptoms-like-drug -addicts-kept-away-tech-gadgets.html.

p. 155, *... pioneering meditation program for its inmates.* Debbie Elliott, "At End-of-the-line Prison, An Unlikely Escape," *NPR,* February 8, 2011, http://www.npr .org/2011/02/08/133505880/at-end-of-the-line-prison-an-unlikely-escape.

p. 155, *In 2008, neuroscientists wired up...* Dian Land, "Study Shows Compassion Meditation Changes the Brain," University of Wisconsin-Madison, March 25, 2008, http://news.wisc.edu/study-shows-compassion-meditation-changes-the-brain/.

p. 158, *Research has shown that...* Netta Weinstein, Andrew K. Przybylski, and Richard M. Ryan, "Can Nature Make Us More Caring? Effects of Immersion in Nature on Intrinsic Aspirations and Generosity," *Personality and Social Psychology Bulletin* 35, no. 10 (2009): 1315–1329.

Guide for Self-Reflection

p. 173, *What has worked well for me...* The ORID method was developed by Canada's Institute for Cultural Affairs for use in facilitated group discussions, but it can also be used for guided self-reflection. For more information, see: Brian Stanfield, *The Art of Focused Conversation: 100 Ways to Access Group Wisdom in the Workplace.* Gabriola Island, BC: New Society Publishers, 2000.

ACKNOWLEDGMENTS

//

I WANT TO THANK THE TEAM AT WONDERWELL. MAGGIE LANGRICK, you're a fantastic publisher to work with. You saw the book's potential from the very beginning and deftly guided its development every step of the way. Joanna Henry, thanks for your steadfast encouragement and excellent edits. I also thank the rest of my production team at Wonderwell.

I owe particular thanks to my friend and writing hero, Carolyn Affleck, for helping to improve the stories I've told here. I also thank Jessica Barrett for your comments and suggestions shaping early drafts of the manuscript.

As well, I offer my gratitude to all the students who have participated in my Project Change course over the years. Your enthusiasm, creativity, and many accomplishments propelled me to keep teaching (and improving) the course. This book wouldn't exist without your inspiration and involvement!

I am also indebted to the numerous individuals who are featured in this book. Thank you for your generosity, time, and patience in responding to my endless questions.

Finally, special thanks are owed to my family and friends for your unwavering support, positivity, and good humor throughout this project.

ABOUT THE AUTHOR

Author photo: Neil Goodes

JOE KELLY is an educator, consultant, and innovator working in sustainability and social change. He teaches university courses and corporate workshops on thinking and acting like a change-maker and has authored numerous articles in mainstream media and academic journals, as well as speaking to audiences around the globe. Joe's professional career encompasses twenty years of experience providing consulting and advisory services to a wide range of businesses, governments, and nonprofit organizations. He holds a PhD in Resource and Environmental Management and is the founder of the Project Change Foundation, a public foundation that provides financial and other support to early-stage charities in Canada with significant potential for creating social or environmental change.